FREE LOOPS

After working in Back or Front Loops Only on a row or round, there will be a ridge of unused loops. These are called the free loops. Later, when instructed to work in the free loops of the same row or round, work in these loops *(Fig. 3a)*.

When instructed to work in free loops of a chain, work in loop indicated by arrow *(Fig. 3b)*.

Fig. 3a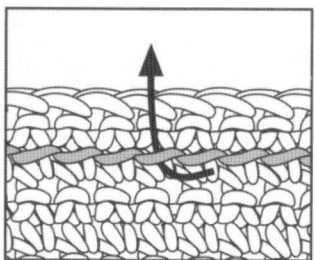

Fig. 3b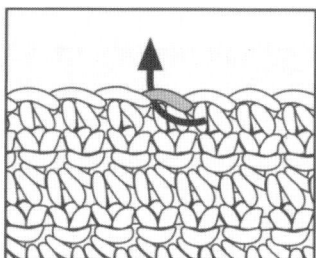

POST STITCH

Work around post of st indicated, inserting hook in direction of arrow *(Fig. 4)*.

Fig. 4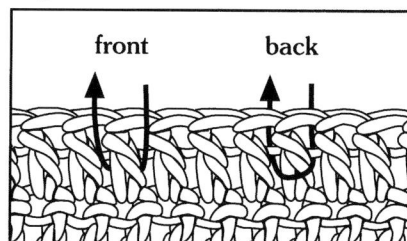

WHIPS'

Place two Squ through both seam, leaving the needle from front to back through **both** loops on **both** pieces *(Fig. 5a)* or through **inside** loops of each stitch on **both** pieces *(Fig. 5b)*, ★ insert the needle from front to back through next stitch and pull yarn through; repeat from ★ across.

Fig. 5a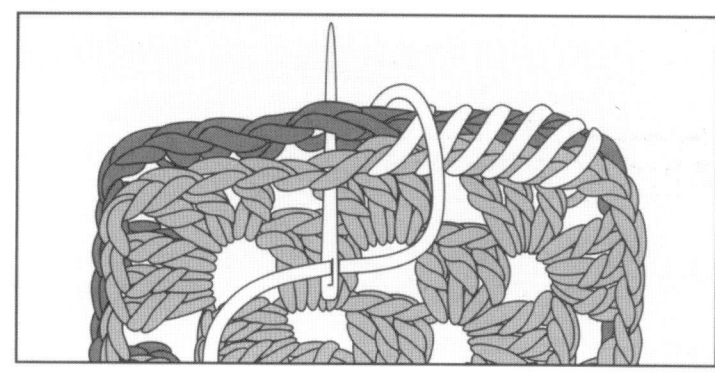

Fig. 5b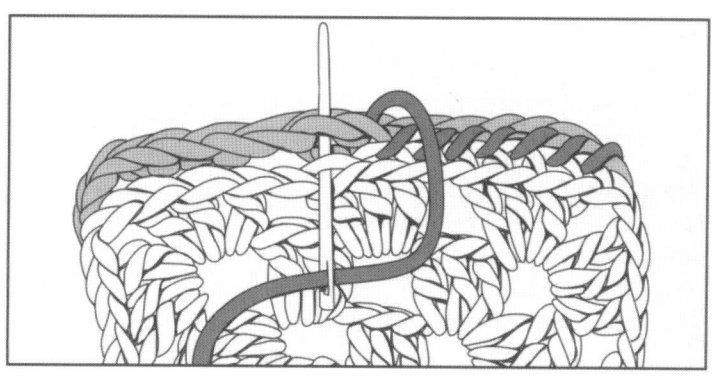

CROCHET TERMINOLOGY	
UNITED STATES	**INTERNATIONAL**
slip stitch (slip st)	= single crochet (sc)
single crochet (sc)	= double crochet (dc)
half double crochet (hdc)	= half treble crochet (htr)
double crochet (dc)	= treble crochet (tr)
treble crochet (tr)	= double treble crochet (dtr)
double treble crochet (dtr)	= triple treble crochet (ttr)
skip	= miss

ALUMINUM CROCHET HOOKS												
U.S.	B-1	C-2	D-3	E-4	F-5	G-6	H-8	I-9	J-10	K-10½	N	P	Q
Metric - mm	2.25	2.75	3.25	3.50	3.75	4.00	5.00	5.50	6.00	6.50	9.00	10.00	15.00

We have made every effort to ensure that these instructions are accurate and complete. We cannot, however, be responsible for human error, typographical mistakes, or variations in individual work.

Afghans and Squares made and instructions tested by Belinda Baxter, Pam Bland, Lee Ellis, Freda Gillham, JoAnn Gonyea, Naomi Greening, Kay Meadors, Margie Norris, Karan Stewart, Clare Stringer, and Margaret Taverner.

1

Finished Size: 44" x 60"

MATERIALS
Worsted Weight Yarn:
- White - 22 ounces, (620 grams, 1,245 yards)
- Purple - 15½ ounces, (440 grams, 875 yards)
- Yellow - 14½ ounces, (410 grams, 820 yards)
- Green - 10 ounces, (280 grams, 565 yards)
- Pink - 9 ounces, (260 grams, 510 yards)

Crochet hook, size G (4.00 mm) **or** size needed for gauge
Safety pins
Yarn needle

GAUGE: Each Lattice Strip = 7"w x 1¼"h
Each Square = 8¼"

Gauge Swatch: 7"w x 1¼"h
Work same as Lattice Strip.

STITCH GUIDE

TREBLE CROCHET (abbreviated tr)
YO twice, insert hook in sc indicated, YO and pull up a loop (4 loops on hook), (YO and draw through 2 loops on hook) 3 times.

SQUARE (Make 35)
LATTICE STRIP

Note: For **each** Square make the number of Lattice Strips indicated in the following colors: Yellow - 3, Purple - 3, Pink - 2, Green - 2.

With color indicated, ch 26 **loosely**.

Row 1 (Right side)**:** Sc in back ridge of second ch from hook and in each ch across *(Fig. 1, page 1)*: 25 sc.

Note: Loop a short piece of yarn around any stitch to mark Row 1 as **right** side.

Row 2: Ch 4 (**counts as first dc plus ch 1, now and throughout**), turn; skip next sc, dc in next sc, ★ ch 1, skip next sc, dc in next sc; repeat from ★ across: 13 dc and 12 ch-1 sps.

Row 3: Ch 1, turn; sc in each dc and in each ch across; finish off: 25 sc.

With **right** sides facing, using photo as a guide for placement, and using safety pins to hold Strips in place, weave Lattice Strips together to form Square.

BORDER

Note: Rnd 1 of Border is worked in end of rows on short edges of Lattice Strips; be careful not to catch stitches on long edges of Strips as you work.

Rnd 1: With **right** side facing, join White with sc in first row on Strip at top right corner *(see Joining With Sc, page 1)*; work 3 sc evenly spaced across Strip, (ch 1, work 4 sc evenly spaced across next Strip) 4 times, ch 3, ★ work 4 sc evenly spaced across next Strip, (ch 1, work 4 sc evenly spaced across next Strip) 4 times, ch 3; repeat from ★ 2 times **more**; join with slip st to first sc: 80 sc and 20 sps.

Rnd 2: Ch 1, sc in Back Loop Only of same st *(Fig. 2, page 1)* and in each sc and in top loop and back ridge of each ch around working 3 sc in center ch of each corner ch-3; join with slip st to first sc: 116 sc.

Rnd 3: Ch 1, sc in Back Loop Only of same st and in each sc around working 3 sc in center sc of each corner 3-sc group; join with slip st to **both** loops of first sc, finish off: 124 sc.

ASSEMBLY

With White and working through **inside** loops only, whipstitch Squares together forming 5 vertical strips of 7 Squares each *(Fig. 5b, page 2)*, beginning in center sc of first corner 3-sc group and ending in center sc of next corner 3-sc group; then whipstitch strips together in same manner.

EDGING

Rnd 1: With **right** side facing and working in Back Loops Only, join White with sc in center sc of any corner 3-sc group; sc in same st, ★ † 2 sc in next sc, sc in next 29 sc, (sc in same st as joining on same Square and in same st as joining on next Square, sc in next 30 sc) across to center sc of next corner 3-sc group †, 3 sc in center sc; repeat from ★ 2 times **more**, then repeat from † to † once, sc in same st as first sc; join with slip st to **both** loops of first sc, do **not** finish off: 776 sc.

Continued on page 43.

First Prize

Laurie Halama

Laurie Halama of Wisconsin, our First Prize winner, became hooked on crochet at the age of 10. After her grandmother taught her how to make a chain stitch, she says, "I immediately fell in love with this craft and begged to learn more!" Laurie has been designing crochet patterns for about three years and loves to make baby clothes, afghans, and doilies. In what little spare time she has from her full-time job at the county courthouse, her family responsibilities, and her crochet projects, she also enjoys cross stitch, sewing, and entering sweepstakes. Laurie and her husband, Scott, have two children: Kaylyn, 6, and Austin, 4.

2

Finished Size: 50" x 66"

MATERIALS
Worsted Weight Yarn:
  Red - 28½ ounces, (810 grams, 1,610 yards)
  White - 21 ounces, (600 grams, 1,190 yards)
  Blue - 11 ounces, (310 grams, 620 yards)
Crochet hook, size H (5.00 mm) **or** size needed for gauge
Yarn needle

GAUGE: Each Square = 8"

Gauge Swatch: 4"w x 2"h
Ch 15 **loosely**.
Row 1: Sc in second ch from hook and in each ch across: 14 sc.
Rows 2-8: Ch 1, turn; sc in each sc across.
Finish off.

STITCH GUIDE

PUFF STITCH (abbreviated Puff St)
★ YO, insert hook in st indicated, YO and pull up a loop; repeat from ★ once **more**, YO and draw through all 5 loops on hook.

SQUARE (Make 48)
CENTER
With Blue, ch 6 **loosely**, drop Blue, with Red, YO and draw through loop on hook, ch 13 **loosely**: 20 chs.

Note: To change colors, work last st to within one step of completion, hook new yarn and draw through all loops on hook. Do not cut yarn unless otherwise instructed.

Row 1: Sc in second ch from hook and in next 11 chs changing to Blue in last sc, sc in last 7 chs: 19 sc.

Note: Continue to change colors in same manner.

Row 2 (Right side)**:** Ch 1, turn; sc in first 7 sc, with Red sc in last 12 sc changing to White in last sc.

*Note: Loop a short piece of yarn around any stitch to mark Row 2 as **right** side and top edge.*

Row 3: Ch 1, turn; sc in first 12 sc, with Blue sc in last 7 sc.

Row 4: Ch 1, turn; sc in first 7 sc, with White sc in last 12 sc changing to Red in last sc.

Row 5: Ch 1, turn; sc in first 12 sc, with Blue sc in last 7 sc.

Row 6: Ch 1, turn; sc in first 7 sc, with Red sc in last 12 sc changing to White in last sc.

Rows 7-10: Repeat Rows 3-6.

Cut Blue.

Row 11: Ch 1, turn; sc in each sc across.

Row 12: Ch 1, turn; sc in each sc across changing to Red in last sc.

Row 13: Ch 1, turn; sc in each sc across.

Row 14: Ch 1, turn; sc in each sc across changing to White in last sc.

Rows 15-21: Repeat Rows 11-14 once, then repeat Rows 11-13 once **more**.

Cut White.

Row 22: Ch 1, turn; sc in each sc across; finish off.

BORDER
Rnd 1: With **right** side facing, join Blue with sc in last sc on Row 22 *(see Joining With Sc, page 1)*; 2 sc in same st, work 17 sc evenly spaced across end of rows; working in free loops of beginning ch *(Fig. 3b, page 2)*, 3 sc in ch at base of first sc, sc in each ch across to last ch, 3 sc in last ch; work 17 sc evenly spaced across end of rows; working in sts across Row 22, 3 sc in first sc, sc in next sc and in each sc across; join with slip st to first sc, finish off: 80 sc.

Rnd 2: With **right** side facing, join White with slip st in center sc of any corner 3-sc group; ch 1, work (Puff St, ch 2, Puff St) in same st, ch 1, skip next sc, (work Puff St in next sc, ch 1, skip next sc) across to center sc of next corner 3-sc group, ★ work (Puff St, ch 2, Puff St) in center sc, ch 1, skip next sc, (work Puff St in next sc, ch 1, skip next sc) across to center sc of next corner 3-sc group; repeat from ★ 2 times **more**; join with slip st to top of first Puff St, finish off: 44 sps.

Rnd 3: With **right** side facing, join Red with slip st in any corner ch-2 sp; ch 2 **(counts as first hdc, now and throughout)**, 4 hdc in same sp, ★ 2 hdc in each ch-1 sp across to next corner ch-2 sp, 5 hdc in corner ch-2 sp; repeat from ★ 2 times **more**, 2 hdc in each ch-1 sp across; join with slip st to first hdc, finish off: 100 hdc.

Continued on page 43.

Second Prize

Nanette M. Seale

Nanette M. Seale of Arizona won Second Prize for her flag-inspired motif. Otherwise left-handed, Nanette learned to crochet right-handed from a woman she met on a camping trip when she was 11. Today she considers it the perfect craft for fulfilling her creative endeavors. "I can do anything with it!" she says. "And I can take it with me. My motto is 'Have crochet, will travel.' " Nanette started designing her own patterns while waiting for the third of her four children to be born. Numerous designs have been published, including some exquisite thread angels in Leisure Arts leaflet #1471, *Heavenly Angels to Crochet*.

3

Finished Size: 51" x 67"

MATERIALS
Worsted Weight Yarn:
  Blue - 33 ounces, (940 grams, 1,865 yards)
  Ecru - 32 ounces, (910 grams, 1,810 yards)
Crochet hook, size H (5.00 mm) **or** size needed for gauge
Yarn needle

GAUGE: Each Square = 8"

Gauge Swatch: 3¼" square
Work same as Square through Rnd 3.

STITCH GUIDE

CLUSTER (uses one st)
YO twice, insert hook from **front** to **back** around post of dc indicated *(Fig. 4, page 2)*, YO and pull up a loop, YO, insert hook from **front** to **back** around post of same st, YO and pull up a loop, YO and draw through 4 loops on hook, (YO and draw through 2 loops on hook) twice. Skip dc behind Cluster.

SQUARE (Make 48)

Rnd 1 (Right side)**:** With Ecru, ch 2, 12 sc in second ch from hook; join with slip st to first sc.

Note: Loop a short piece of yarn around any stitch to mark Rnd 1 as **right** side.

Rnd 2: Ch 6, working in Back Loops Only *(Fig. 2, page 1)*, (dc in next 3 sc, ch 3) 3 times, dc in last 2 sc; join with slip st to third ch of beginning ch-6: 12 sts and 4 ch-3 sps.

Rnd 3: Ch 3 **(counts as first dc, now and throughout)**, working in Back Loops Only, dc in next ch, (dc, ch 3, dc) in next ch, dc in next ch, ★ dc in next 3 dc and in next ch, (dc, ch 3, dc) in next ch, dc in next ch; repeat from ★ 2 times **more**, dc in last 2 dc; join with slip st to first dc, finish off: 28 dc and 4 ch-3 sps.

Rnd 4: With **right** side facing, join Blue with sc in any corner ch-3 sp *(see Joining With Sc, page 1)*; (sc, ch 2, 2 sc) in same sp, working in both loops, sc in next 2 dc, work Cluster around dc one rnd **below** next dc, sc in next dc, work Cluster around dc one rnd **below** next dc, sc in next 2 dc, ★ (2 sc, ch 2, 2 sc) in next corner ch-3 sp, sc in next 2 dc, work Cluster around dc one rnd **below** next dc, sc in next dc, work Cluster around dc one rnd **below** next dc, sc in next 2 dc; repeat from ★ 2 times **more**; join with slip st to first sc, finish off: 44 sts and 4 ch-2 sps.

Rnd 5: With **right** side facing and working in Back Loops Only, join Ecru with dc in first ch of any corner ch-2 *(see Joining With Dc, page 1)*; dc in same ch, ch 3, 2 dc in next ch, dc in next 11 sts, ★ 2 dc in next ch, ch 3, 2 dc in next ch, dc in next 11 sts; repeat from ★ 2 times **more**; join with slip st to Back Loop Only of first dc: 60 dc and 4 ch-3 sps.

Rnd 6: Ch 3, working in Back Loops Only, dc in next dc and in next ch, (dc, ch 3, dc) in next ch, ★ dc in next ch, dc in next 15 dc and in next ch, (dc, ch 3, dc) in next ch; repeat from ★ 2 times **more**, dc in next ch and in last 13 dc; join with slip st to **both** loops of first dc, finish off: 76 dc and 4 ch-3 sps.

Rnd 7: With **right** side facing and working in both loops, join Blue with sc in any corner ch-3 sp; (sc, ch 2, 2 sc) in same sp, sc in next 2 dc, work Cluster around dc one rnd **below** next dc, sc in next dc, work Cluster around dc one rnd **below** next dc, (sc in next 3 dc, work Cluster around dc one rnd **below** next dc, sc in next dc, work Cluster around dc one rnd **below** next dc) twice, sc in next 2 dc, ★ (2 sc, ch 2, 2 sc) in next corner ch-3 sp, sc in next 2 dc, work Cluster around dc one rnd **below** next dc, sc in next dc, work Cluster around dc one rnd **below** next dc, (sc in next 3 dc, work Cluster around dc one rnd **below** next dc, sc in next dc, work Cluster around dc one rnd **below** next dc) twice, sc in next 2 dc; repeat from ★ 2 times **more**; join with slip st to first sc, finish off: 24 Clusters, 68 sc, and 4 ch-2 sps.

Rnd 8: With **right** side facing and working in Back Loops Only, join Ecru with sc in first ch of any corner ch-2; ch 2, sc in next ch and in each st across to next corner ch-2, ★ sc in next ch, ch 2, sc in next ch and in each st across to next corner ch-2; repeat from ★ 2 times **more**; join with slip st to **both** loops of first sc, finish off: 100 sc and 4 ch-2 sps.

Rnd 9: With **right** side facing, join Blue with sc in any corner ch-2 sp; ch 2, sc in same sp, ch 1, skip next sc, working in both loops, ★ (sc in next sc, ch 1, skip next sc) across to next corner ch-2 sp, (sc, ch 2, sc) in corner ch-2 sp, ch 1, skip next sc; repeat from ★ 2 times **more**, (sc in next sc, ch 1, skip next sc) across; join with slip st to first sc, finish off: 56 sc and 56 sps.

Continued on page 43.

Third Prize

Edna L. Neuhart

Edna L. Neuhart of Washington, our Third Prize winner, says she enjoys experimenting with patterns. Having learned from her mother to crochet at age 16, Edna's favorite projects have been afghans, lap robes, and baby coverlets. "Crocheting has brought much pleasure to me over the years by enabling me to make things for my two daughters, three grandchildren, and two great-grandchildren," she says. Edna has given at least 150 of her afghans to family, friends, and fund-raising campaigns. "I'm grateful for the ability to make and give afghans — lasting gifts which cannot be purchased in ordinary retail stores," she says.

4

Finished Size: 51" x 67"

MATERIALS
Worsted Weight Yarn:
   61 ounces, (1,730 grams, 3,450 yards)
Crochet hook, size H (5.00 mm) **or** size needed
   for gauge
Yarn needle

GAUGE: Each Square = 8"

Gauge Swatch: 7"w x 2"h
Work same as Square through Row 3.

STITCH GUIDE

FRONT POST TREBLE CROCHET
(abbreviated FPtr)
YO twice, insert hook from **front** to **back** around post of st indicated *(Fig. 4, page 2)*, YO and pull up a loop (4 loops on hook), (YO and draw through 2 loops on hook) 3 times. Skip st behind FPtr unless otherwise specified.

BACK POST TREBLE CROCHET
(abbreviated BPtr)
YO twice, insert hook from **back** to **front** around post of st indicated *(Fig. 4, page 2)*, YO and pull up a loop (4 loops on hook), (YO and draw through 2 loops on hook) 3 times. Skip st in front of BPtr.

SQUARE (Make 48)
CENTER
Ch 26 **loosely**, place marker in third ch from hook for st placement.

Row 1 (Right side)**:** Dc in fourth ch from hook **(3 skipped chs count as first dc)** and in next ch, ★ (skip next ch, dc in next ch, working **around** last dc made, dc in skipped ch) twice, dc in next 3 chs; repeat from ★ 2 times **more**: 24 dc.

Note: Loop a short piece of yarn around any stitch to mark Row 1 as **right** side and bottom edge.

Row 2: Ch 3 **(counts as first dc, now and throughout)**, turn; work BPtr around next dc, dc in next dc, ★ (skip next dc, dc in next dc, working **around** last dc made, dc in skipped dc) twice, dc in next dc, work BPtr around next dc, dc in next dc; repeat from ★ 2 times **more**: 4 BPtr and 20 dc.

Row 3: Ch 3, turn; work FPtr around next BPtr, dc in next dc, ★ (skip next dc, dc in next dc, working **around** last dc made, dc in skipped dc) twice, dc in next dc, work FPtr around next BPtr, dc in next dc; repeat from ★ 2 times **more**: 4 FPtr and 20 dc.

Row 4: Ch 3, turn; work BPtr around next FPtr, dc in next dc, ★ (skip next dc, dc in next dc, working **around** last dc made, dc in skipped dc) twice, dc in next dc, work BPtr around next FPtr, dc in next dc; repeat from ★ 2 times **more**: 4 BPtr and 20 dc.

Rows 5-11: Repeat Rows 3 and 4, 3 times; then repeat Row 3 once **more**; do **not** finish off.

BORDER
Rnd 1: Ch 1, do **not** turn; 2 sc in end of each row across; working in free loops of beginning ch *(Fig. 3b, page 2)*, 3 sc in first ch, sc in next ch and in each ch across to marked ch, 3 sc in marked ch; 2 sc in end of each row across; working in sts across Row 11, 3 sc in first dc, sc in next 22 sts, 3 sc in last dc; join with slip st to first sc: 100 sc.

Rnd 2: Ch 1, sc in each sc around working 3 sc in center sc of each corner 3-sc group; join with slip st to first sc, finish off: 108 sc.

ASSEMBLY
Using photo as a guide, alternating bottom of Squares, and working through **both** loops, whipstitch Squares together forming 6 vertical strips of 8 Squares each *(Fig. 5a, page 2)*, beginning in center sc of first corner 3-sc group and ending in center sc of next corner 3-sc group; then whipstitch strips together in same manner.

Continued on page 44.

5

Finished Size: 52" x 68"

MATERIALS
Worsted Weight Yarn:
    White - 28 ounces, (800 grams, 1,585 yards)
    Blue - 27 ounces, (770 grams, 1,525 yards)
    Lt Blue - 22½ ounces, (640 grams, 1,270 yards)
Crochet hook, size G (4.00 mm) **or** size needed
    for gauge
Yarn needle

GAUGE: Each Square = 8"

Gauge Swatch: 3" diameter
Work same as Square A through Rnd 2.

STITCH GUIDE

TREBLE CROCHET *(abbreviated tr)*
YO twice, insert hook in st indicated, YO and pull up a loop (4 loops on hook), (YO and draw through 2 loops on hook) 3 times.

DOUBLE TREBLE CROCHET
   (abbreviated dtr)
YO 3 times, insert hook in st indicated, YO and pull up a loop (5 loops on hook), (YO and draw through 2 loops on hook) 4 times.

FRONT POST DOUBLE CROCHET
   (abbreviated FPdc)
YO, insert hook from **front** to **back** around post of st indicated *(Fig. 4, page 2)*, YO and pull up a loop (3 loops on hook), (YO and draw through 2 loops on hook) twice. Skip st behind FPdc.

BEGINNING BACK POST DOUBLE
   CROCHET *(abbreviated Beginning BPdc)*
Insert hook from **back** to **front** around post of same st *(Fig. 4, page 2)*, YO and draw through loop on hook, ch 3. Skip st in front of BPdc.

BACK POST DOUBLE CROCHET
   (abbreviated BPdc)
YO, insert hook from **back** to **front** around post of st indicated *(Fig. 4, page 2)*, YO and pull up a loop (3 loops on hook), (YO and draw through 2 loops on hook) twice. Skip st in front of BPdc.

CLUSTER (uses next 3 sts)
★ YO, insert hook from **front** to **back** around post of **next** st *(Fig. 4, page 2)*, YO and pull up a loop, YO and draw through 2 loops on hook; repeat from ★ 2 times **more**, YO and draw through all 4 loops on hook.

STAR (uses next 7 sts)
Pull up a loop in each of next 3 dc, skip next sc, pull up a loop in each of next 3 dc, YO and draw through all 7 loops on hook.

SQUARE A (Make 24)

Rnd 1 (Right side)**:** With Blue, ch 5, 23 tr in fifth ch from hook **(4 skipped chs count as first tr)**; join with slip st to first tr: 24 tr.

Note: Loop a short piece of yarn around any stitch to mark Rnd 1 as **right** side.

Rnd 2: Work Beginning BPdc, work 2 FPdc around next tr, work (BPdc around next tr, 2 FPdc around next tr) around; join with slip st to Beginning BPdc: 36 sts.

Rnd 3: Work Beginning BPdc, work FPdc around next FPdc, dc in sp **before** next FPdc, work FPdc around next FPdc, ★ work BPdc around next BPdc, work FPdc around next FPdc, dc in sp **before** next FPdc, work FPdc around next FPdc; repeat from ★ around; join with slip st to Beginning BPdc: 48 sts.

Rnd 4: Insert hook from **back** to **front** around post of same st, YO and draw through loop on hook, ch 5 **(counts as Beginning BPdc plus ch 2)**, work Cluster, ch 2, ★ work BPdc around next BPdc, ch 2, work Cluster, ch 2; repeat from ★ around; join with slip st to Beginning BPdc, finish off: 24 ch-2 sps.

Rnd 5: With **right** side facing, join White with dc in first ch-2 sp *(see Joining With Dc, page 1)*; 3 dc in same sp, 2 dc in each of next 4 ch-2 sps, 4 dc in next ch-2 sp, ch 2, ★ 4 dc in next ch-2 sp, 2 dc in each of next 4 ch-2 sps, 4 dc in next ch-2 sp, ch 2; repeat from ★ 2 times **more**; join with slip st to first dc: 64 dc and 4 ch-2 sps.

Rnd 6: Ch 1, sc in same st and in each dc across to next corner ch-2 sp, 3 sc in corner ch-2 sp, ★ sc in each dc across to next corner ch-2 sp, 3 sc in corner ch-2 sp; repeat from ★ 2 times **more**; join with slip st to first sc, finish off: 76 sc.

Continued on page 44.

6

Finished Size: 50" x 66"

MATERIALS
Worsted Weight Yarn:
  White - 33 ounces, (940 grams, 1,865 yards)
  Green - 21 ounces, (600 grams, 1,190 yards)
  Blue - 2 ounces, (60 grams, 115 yards)
  Yellow - 2 ounces, (60 grams, 115 yards)
  Rose - 2 ounces, (60 grams, 115 yards)
  Purple - 2 ounces, (60 grams, 115 yards)
Crochet hook, size I (5.50 mm) **or** size needed for gauge
Yarn needle

GAUGE: Each Square = 8"

Gauge Swatch: 2¾" diameter
Work same as Flower through Rnd 2.

STITCH GUIDE

TREBLE CROCHET *(abbreviated tr)*
YO twice, insert hook in st indicated, YO and pull up a loop (4 loops on hook), (YO and draw through 2 loops on hook) 3 times.

SQUARE (Make 48)
FLOWER
Note: Make 12 Flowers **each** in the following colors: Blue, Yellow, Rose, and Purple.

With color indicated, ch 5; join with slip st to form a ring.

Rnd 1 (Right side)**:** Ch 3 **(counts as first dc, now and throughout)**, 2 dc in ring, ch 1, (3 dc in ring, ch 1) 4 times; join with slip st to first dc: 15 dc and 5 ch-1 sps.

Note: Loop a short piece of yarn around any stitch to mark Rnd 1 as **right** side.

Rnd 2: Ch 2 **(counts as first hdc)**, dc in next dc, hdc in next dc, ch 2, ★ hdc in next dc, dc in next dc, hdc in next dc, ch 2; repeat from ★ around; join with slip st to first hdc: 15 sts and 5 ch-2 sps.

Rnd 3: Ch 3, working in Front Loops Only *(Fig. 2, page 1)*, dc in same st, 2 tr in next dc, 2 dc in next hdc, working **around** next ch-2, sc in ch one rnd **below** (petal made), ★ 2 dc in next hdc, 2 tr in next dc, 2 dc in next hdc, working **around** next ch-2, sc in ch one rnd **below** (petal made); repeat from ★ around; join with slip st to first dc, finish off: 5 petals.

LEAVES
Rnd 1: With **right** side facing, working **behind** petals and in free loops on Rnds 1 and 2 *(Fig. 3a, page 2)*, join Green with slip st in any ch on Rnd 1; ch 7, (2 tr, ch 4, slip st) in fifth ch from hook, slip st in next 3 sts on Rnd 2, dc in next ch on Rnd 1, (slip st, ch 4, 2 tr, ch 4, slip st) in next st on Rnd 2, slip st in next 2 sts, dc in next ch on Rnd 1, slip st in next st on Rnd 2, (slip st, ch 4, 2 tr, ch 4, slip st) in next st, slip st in next st, dc in next ch on Rnd 1, slip st in next 2 sts on Rnd 2, (slip st, ch 4, 2 tr, ch 4, slip st) in next st, dc in next ch on Rnd 1, slip st in last 3 sts on Rnd 2; join with slip st to third ch of beginning ch-7.

Rnd 2: Ch 1, ★ 4 sc in next ch-4 sp, skip next tr, working in both loops, 2 sc in next tr, 4 sc in next ch-4 sp, skip next slip st, sc in next 4 sts; repeat from ★ around; join with slip st to first sc, finish off: 56 sc.

BORDER
Rnd 1: With **right** side facing, join White with sc in second sc of 2-sc group at tip of any Leaf *(see Joining With Sc, page 1)*; sc in next 2 sc, hdc in next sc, dc in next 6 sc, hdc in next sc, sc in next 3 sc, ch 2, ★ sc in next 3 sc, hdc in next sc, dc in next 6 sc, hdc in next sc, sc in next 3 sc, ch 2; repeat from ★ 2 times **more**; join with slip st to first sc: 56 sts and 4 ch-2 sps.

Rnd 2: Ch 1, sc in same st and in each st across to next corner ch-2 sp, 2 sc in corner ch-2 sp, (sc in each st across to next corner ch-2 sp, 2 sc in corner ch-2 sp) around; join with slip st to first sc, finish off: 64 sc.

Continued on page 45.

7

Finished Size: 55" x 72½"

MATERIALS
Worsted Weight Yarn:
    Purple - 29 ounces, (820 grams, 1,640 yards)
    Brown - 28 ounces, (800 grams, 1,585 yards)
    Rose - 26 ounces, (740 grams, 1,470 yards)
    Teal - 23 ounces, (650 grams, 1,300 yards)
Crochet hook, size F (3.75 mm) **or** size needed for gauge
Yarn needle

GAUGE: Each Square = 8¾"

Gauge Swatch: 8¾"w x 2¼"h
Work same as Square through Row 6.

STITCH GUIDE

LONG SINGLE CROCHET (abbreviated LSC)
Working **around** last 3 dc made, insert hook in skipped sc, YO and pull up a loop even with last st made, YO and draw through both loops on hook.

RIB
★ YO, insert hook from **front** to **back** around post of st indicated *(Fig. 4, page 2)*, YO and pull up a loop; repeat from ★ once **more**, YO and draw through all 5 loops on hook. Skip st behind Rib.

POPCORN
3 Dc in st indicated, drop loop from hook, insert hook in first dc of 3-dc group, hook dropped loop and draw through, ch 1 to close.

SQUARE (Make 48)
With Teal, ch 35 **loosely**.

Row 1 (Right side)**:** Sc in back ridge of second ch from hook and each ch across *(Fig. 1, page 1)*: 34 sc.

Note: Loop a short piece of yarn around any stitch to mark Row 1 as **right** side and bottom edge.

Row 2: Ch 3 (counts as first dc, now and throughout), turn; ★ skip next sc, dc in next 3 sc, work LSC; repeat from ★ across to last sc, dc in last sc: 8 LSC.

Row 3: Ch 1, turn; sc in each st across: 34 sc.

Row 4: Ch 3, turn; ★ skip next sc, dc in next 3 sc, work LSC; repeat from ★ across to last sc, dc in last sc.

Rows 5 and 6: Repeat Rows 3 and 4.

Finish off.

Row 7: With **wrong** side facing, join Purple with sc in first dc *(see Joining With Sc, page 1)*; sc in next dc and in each st across: 34 sc.

Row 8: Ch 1, turn; sc in first 3 sc, work Rib around next sc, (sc in next 2 sc, work Rib around next sc) across to last 3 sc, sc in last 3 sc: 10 Ribs.

Row 9: Ch 1, turn; sc in each st across: 34 sc.

Row 10: Ch 1, turn; sc in first 3 sc, work Rib around Rib one row **below** next sc, (sc in next 2 sc, work Rib around Rib one row **below** next sc) across to last 3 sc, sc in last 3 sc: 10 Ribs.

Rows 11-16: Repeat Rows 9 and 10, 3 times.

Finish off.

Row 17: With **wrong** side facing, join Rose with sc in first sc; dc in next sc, (sc in next st, dc in next st) across: 34 sts.

Rows 18-24: Ch 1, turn; sc in first dc, dc in next sc, (sc in next dc, dc in next sc) across.

Finish off.

Row 25: With **wrong** side facing, join Brown with sc in first dc; sc in next sc and in each st across.

Row 26: Ch 1, turn; sc in first 2 sc, (work Popcorn in next sc, sc in next 3 sc) across: 8 Popcorns.

Row 27: Ch 1, turn; sc in each st across: 34 sc.

Row 28: Ch 1, turn; sc in first 4 sc, work Popcorn in next sc, (sc in next 3 sc, work Popcorn in next sc) across to last 5 sc, sc in last 5 sc: 7 Popcorns.

Row 29: Ch 1, turn; sc in each st across: 34 sc.

Rows 30-33: Repeat Rows 26-29.

Finish off.

ASSEMBLY
With desired color, using photo as a guide, alternating bottom of Squares, and working through **both** loops of sts and in end of rows, sew Squares together forming 6 vertical strips of 8 Squares each; then sew strips together.

Continued on page 45.

15

8

Finished Size: 51" x 67"

MATERIALS
Worsted Weight Yarn:
  Ecru - 40½ ounces, (1,150 grams, 2,290 yards)
  Green - 27½ ounces, (780 grams, 1,555 yards)
Crochet hook, size I (5.50 mm) **or** size needed for gauge
Yarn needle

GAUGE: Each Square = 8"

Gauge Swatch: 3¼" square
Work same as Square through Rnd 3.

STITCH GUIDE

FRONT POST TREBLE CROCHET
  (abbreviated FPtr)
YO twice, insert hook from **front** to **back** around post of st indicated *(Fig. 4, page 2)*, YO and pull up a loop (4 loops on hook), (YO and draw through 2 loops on hook) 3 times. Skip st behind FPtr.

SQUARE (Make 48)
With Green, ch 6; join with slip st to form a ring.

Rnd 1 (Right side)**:** Ch 1, (3 sc in ring, ch 4) 4 times; join with slip st to first sc: 12 sc and 4 ch-4 sps.

Note: Loop a short piece of yarn around any stitch to mark Rnd 1 as **right** side.

Rnd 2: Ch 1, sc in same st and in next 2 sc, (slip st, ch 9, slip st) in next ch-4 sp, ★ sc in next 3 sc, (slip st, ch 9, slip st) in next ch-4 sp; repeat from ★ 2 times **more**; join with slip st to first sc, finish off.

Rnd 3: With **right** side facing and working **behind** corner ch-9, join Ecru with slip st in any corner ch-4 sp on Rnd 1 (between slip sts); ch 3 **(counts as first dc, now and throughout)**, (dc, ch 2, 2 dc) in same sp, dc in next 3 sc on Rnd 2, ★ working **behind** next corner ch-9, (2 dc, ch 2, 2 dc) in corner ch-4 sp on Rnd 1 (between slip sts), dc in next 3 sc on Rnd 2; repeat from ★ 2 times **more**; join with slip st to first dc: 28 dc and 4 ch-2 sps.

Rnd 4: Ch 3, dc in next dc, ★ † 2 dc in next ch-2 sp, (dc, ch 9, slip st in top of dc just made, dc) in next ch-9 sp on Rnd 2, 2 dc in same sp on Rnd 3, dc in next 2 dc, ch 3, skip next 3 dc †, dc in next 2 dc; repeat from ★ 2 times **more**, then repeat from † to † once; join with slip st to first dc, finish off: 40 dc and 8 sps.

Rnd 5: With **right** side facing, join Green with slip st in same st as joining; ch 3, dc in next 3 dc, ★ † 2 dc in next dc, ch 1, working **behind** next ch-9, 2 dc in next dc, dc in next 4 dc, work FPtr around each of next 3 dc one rnd **below** next ch-3 †, dc in next 4 dc; repeat from ★ 2 times **more**, then repeat from † to † once; join with slip st to first dc: 60 sts and 4 ch-1 sps.

Rnd 6: Ch 3, dc in next 5 dc, ★ † (2 dc, ch 9, slip st in top of last dc made, 2 dc) in next ch-9 sp on Rnd 4, dc in next 6 dc on Rnd 5, work FPtr around each of next 3 FPtr †, dc in next 6 dc; repeat from ★ 2 times **more**, then repeat from † to † once; join with slip st to first dc, finish off: 76 sts and 4 ch-9 sps.

Rnd 7: With **right** side facing, join Ecru with slip st in same st as joining; ch 3, dc in next 6 dc, ★ † 2 dc in next dc, ch 2, working **behind** next ch-9, 2 dc in next dc †, dc in next 17 sts; repeat from ★ 2 times **more**, then repeat from † to † once, dc in last 10 sts; join with slip st to first dc: 84 dc and 4 ch-2 sps.

Rnd 8: Ch 1, sc in same st and in next 8 dc, 3 sc in next ch-9 sp on Rnd 6, (sc in next 21 dc on Rnd 7, 3 sc in next ch-9 sp on Rnd 6) 3 times, sc in last 12 dc; join with slip st to first sc, finish off: 96 sc.

ASSEMBLY
With Ecru and working through **both** loops, whipstitch Squares together forming 6 vertical strips of 8 Squares each *(Fig. 5a, page 2)*, beginning in center sc of first corner 3-sc group and ending in center sc of next corner 3-sc group; then whipstitch strips together in same manner.

Continued on page 46.

9

Finished Size: 51½" x 67½"

MATERIALS
Worsted Weight Yarn:
  65 ounces, (1,850 grams, 3,675 yards)
Crochet hook, size D (3.25 mm) **or** size needed
  for gauge
Yarn needle

GAUGE: Each Square = 8"

Gauge Swatch: 3¼" diameter
Work same as Square through Rnd 3.

STITCH GUIDE

TREBLE CROCHET *(abbreviated tr)*
YO twice, insert hook in st indicated, YO and pull up a loop (4 loops on hook), (YO and draw through 2 loops on hook) 3 times.

SQUARE (Make 48)
Ch 7; join with slip st to form a ring.

Rnd 1 (Right side)**:** Ch 6, dc in ring, (ch 3, dc in ring) 6 times, ch 1, hdc in third ch of beginning ch-6 to form last ch-3 sp: 8 ch-3 sps.

Note: Loop a short piece of yarn around any stitch to mark Rnd 1 as **right** side.

Rnd 2: Ch 1, sc in same sp, (ch 7, sc in next ch-3 sp) around, ch 3, tr in first sc to form last ch-7 sp.

Rnd 3: Ch 1, sc in same sp, ch 6, (sc in next ch-7 sp, ch 6) around; join with slip st to first sc.

Rnd 4: Ch 1, sc in same st, 6 sc in next ch-6 sp, (sc in next sc, 6 sc in next ch-6 sp) around; join with slip st to first sc: 56 sc.

Rnd 5: Ch 3 **(counts as first dc, now and throughout)**, dc in same st and in next 6 sc, (2 dc in next sc, dc in next 6 sc) around; join with slip st to first dc: 64 dc.

Rnd 6: Ch 1, 2 sc in same st, sc in next 7 dc, (2 sc in next dc, sc in next 7 dc) around; join with slip st to first sc: 72 sc.

Rnd 7: Ch 1, sc in same st, ★ ch 3, skip next sc, sc in next sc; repeat from ★ around to last sc, ch 1, skip last sc, hdc in first sc to form last ch-3 sp: 36 ch-3 sps.

Rnd 8: Ch 1, sc in same sp, (ch 4, sc in next ch-3 sp) around, tr in first sc to form last ch-4 sp.

Rnd 9: Ch 3, (2 dc, ch 3, 3 dc) in same sp, ch 3, skip next ch-4 sp, (sc in next ch-4 sp, ch 3) 6 times, skip next ch-4 sp, ★ (3 dc, ch 3) twice in next ch-4 sp, skip next ch-4 sp, (sc in next ch-4 sp, ch 3) 6 times, skip next ch-4 sp; repeat from ★ 2 times **more**; join with slip st to first dc: 32 ch-3 sps.

Rnd 10: Slip st in next 2 dc and in next corner ch-3 sp, ch 3, (2 dc, ch 3, 3 dc) in same sp, ch 3, dc in next ch-3 sp, ch 3, (sc in next ch-3 sp, ch 3) 5 times, dc in next ch-3 sp, ch 3, ★ (3 dc, ch 3) twice in next corner ch-3 sp, dc in next ch-3 sp, ch 3, (sc in next ch-3 sp, ch 3) 5 times, dc in next ch-3 sp, ch 3; repeat from ★ 2 times **more**; join with slip st to first dc: 52 sts and 36 ch-3 sps.

Rnd 11: Ch 1, sc in same st and in next 2 dc, 3 sc in next corner ch-3 sp, sc in next 3 dc, 2 sc in next ch-3 sp, (sc in next st, 2 sc in next ch-3 sp) 7 times, ★ sc in next 3 dc, 3 sc in next corner ch-3 sp, sc in next 3 dc, 2 sc in next ch-3 sp, (sc in next st, 2 sc in next ch-3 sp) 7 times; repeat from ★ 2 times **more**; join with slip st to first sc: 128 sc.

Rnd 12: Ch 4 **(counts as first dc plus ch 1, now and throughout)**, skip next sc, dc in next sc, ch 1, skip next sc, (dc, ch 1) 3 times in next sc, skip next sc, ★ (dc in next sc, ch 1, skip next sc) across to center sc of next corner 3-sc group, (dc, ch 1) 3 times in center sc, skip next sc; repeat from ★ 2 times **more**, (dc in next sc, ch 1, skip next sc) across; join with slip st to first dc, finish off: 72 dc and 72 ch-1 sps.

ASSEMBLY
Working through **both** loops, whipstitch Squares together forming 6 vertical strips of 8 Squares each *(Fig. 5a, page 2)*, beginning in center dc of first corner 3-dc group and ending in center dc of next corner 3-dc group; then whipstitch strips together in same manner.

EDGING
Rnd 1: With **right** side facing, join yarn with sc in center dc of any corner *(see Joining With Sc, page 1)*; ch 3, sc in same st, ch 3, ★ (sc in next dc, ch 3) 17 times, † sc in next joining, ch 3, (sc in next dc, ch 3) 17 times †, repeat from † to † across to center dc of next corner, (sc, ch 3) twice in center dc; repeat from ★ 2 times **more**, (sc in next dc, ch 3) 17 times, repeat from † to † across; join with slip st to first sc, do **not** finish off: 508 ch-3 sps.

Continued on page 46.

10

Finished Size: 52½" x 69½"

MATERIALS
Worsted Weight Yarn:
   Rose - 48½ ounces, (1,380 grams, 2,745 yards)
   Ecru - 31½ ounces, (890 grams, 1,780 yards)
Crochet hook, size F (3.75 mm) **or** size needed for gauge
Yarn needle

GAUGE: Each Square = 8½"

Gauge Swatch: 2½" diameter
Work same as Square through Rnd 2.

STITCH GUIDE

TREBLE CROCHET *(abbreviated tr)*
YO twice, insert hook in st indicated, YO and pull up a loop (4 loops on hook), (YO and draw through 2 loops on hook) 3 times.

LOCKED TREBLE CROCHET
(abbreviated Locked tr) (uses next 2 sts)
YO twice, insert hook from **front** to **back** in st indicated, then from **back** to **front** in next st indicated, YO and pull up a loop (4 loops on hook), (YO and draw through 2 loops on hook) 3 times.

CLUSTER *(uses one st)*
★ YO twice, insert hook in st indicated, YO and pull up a loop, (YO and draw through 2 loops on hook) twice; repeat from ★ 2 times **more**, YO and draw through all 4 loops on hook.

SQUARE (Make 48)
With Rose, ch 4; join with slip st to form a ring.

Rnd 1 (Right side)**:** Ch 1, 8 sc in ring; join with slip st to first sc.

Note: Loop a short piece of yarn around any stitch to mark Rnd 1 as **right** side.

Rnd 2: Ch 3, ★ YO twice, insert hook in same st, YO and pull up a loop, (YO and draw through 2 loops on hook) twice; repeat from ★ once **more**, YO and draw through all 3 loops on hook **(Beginning Cluster made)**, ch 3, (work Cluster in next sc, ch 3) around; join with slip st to top of Beginning Cluster, finish off: 8 ch-3 sps.

Rnd 3: With **right** side facing, join Ecru with slip st in any ch-3 sp; ch 3 **(counts as first dc, now and throughout)**, (2 dc, ch 3, 3 dc) in same sp, 3 dc in next ch-3 sp, ★ (3 dc, ch 3, 3 dc) in next ch-3 sp, 3 dc in next ch-3 sp; repeat from ★ 2 times **more**; join with slip st to first dc, finish off: 36 dc and 4 ch-3 sps.

Rnd 4: With **right** side facing, join Rose with slip st in any corner ch-3 sp; ch 3, 2 dc in same sp, (skip next dc, dc in next 2 dc, working in **front** of last 2 dc made, tr in skipped dc) 3 times, ★ (3 dc, ch 3, 3 dc) in next corner ch-3 sp, (skip next dc, dc in next 2 dc, working in **front** of last 2 dc made, tr in skipped dc) 3 times; repeat from ★ 2 times **more**, 3 dc in same sp as first dc, dc in first dc to form last ch-3 sp: 60 sts and 4 ch-3 sps.

Rnd 5: Ch 3, (2 dc, ch 3, 3 dc) in same sp, ★ † skip next 2 dc, work Locked tr in next 2 sts, working **behind** Locked tr, dc in 2 skipped dc, (skip next dc, work Locked tr in next 2 sts, working **behind** Locked tr, dc in same dc as previous Locked tr and in skipped dc) 3 times, skip next dc, work Locked tr in next dc and in first ch of next corner ch-3, working **behind** Locked tr, dc in same dc as previous Locked tr and in skipped dc †, (3 dc, ch 3, 3 dc) in next corner ch-3 sp; repeat from ★ 2 times **more**, then repeat from † to † once; join with slip st to first dc, finish off: 84 sts and 4 ch-3 sps.

Rnd 6: With **right** side facing, join Ecru with slip st in any corner ch-3 sp; ch 3, 2 dc in same sp, (skip next st, dc in next 2 dc, working in **front** of last 2 dc made, tr in skipped st) 7 times, ★ (3 dc, ch 3, 3 dc) in next corner ch-3 sp, (skip next st, dc in next 2 dc, working in **front** of last 2 dc made, tr in skipped st) 7 times; repeat from ★ 2 times **more**, 3 dc in same sp as first dc, dc in first dc to form last ch-3 sp: 108 sts and 4 ch-3 sps.

Rnd 7: Ch 3, (dc, ch 3, 2 dc) in same sp, ★ † skip next 2 dc, work Locked tr in next 2 sts, working **behind** Locked tr, dc in 2 skipped dc, (skip next dc, work Locked tr in next 2 sts, working **behind** Locked tr, dc in same dc as previous Locked tr and in skipped dc) 7 times, skip next dc, work Locked tr in next dc and in first ch of next corner ch-3, working **behind** Locked tr, dc in same dc as previous Locked tr and in skipped dc †, (2 dc, ch 3, 2 dc) in next corner ch-3 sp; repeat from ★ 2 times **more**, then repeat from † to † once; join with slip st to first dc, finish off: 124 sts and 4 ch-3 sps.

Continued on page 46.

11

Finished Size: 8" square

MATERIALS
Worsted Weight Yarn:
- Blue - 28 yards
- Dk Blue - 18 yards
- Red - 7 yards

Crochet hook, size H (5.00 mm) **or** size needed for gauge

GAUGE SWATCH: 1¼" diameter
Work same as Square through Rnd 2.

STITCH GUIDE

BEGINNING CLUSTER (uses one st)
Ch 2, ★ YO, insert hook in **same** st, YO and pull up a loop, YO and draw through 2 loops on hook; repeat from ★ once **more**, YO and draw through all 3 loops on hook.

CLUSTER (uses one st)
★ YO, insert hook in st indicated, YO and pull up a loop, YO and draw through 2 loops on hook; repeat from ★ 2 times **more**, YO and draw through all 4 loops on hook.

With Red, ch 4; join with slip st to form a ring.

Rnd 1 (Right side)**:** Ch 1, 6 sc in ring; join with slip st to first sc.

Note: Loop a short piece of yarn around any stitch to mark Rnd 1 as **right** side.

Rnd 2: Ch 3, (slip st in next sc, ch 3) around; join with slip st to Front Loop Only of joining slip st *(Fig. 2, page 1)*: 6 ch-3 sps.

Rnd 3: Ch 5, working in Front Loops Only, (slip st in next slip st, ch 5) around; join with slip st to **both** loops of joining slip st.

Rnd 4: Ch 9, working in both loops, (slip st in next slip st, ch 9) around; join with slip st to joining slip st.

Rnd 5: Ch 12, (slip st in next slip st, ch 12) around; join with slip st to joining slip st, finish off.

Rnd 6: With **wrong** side facing and working in free loops on Rnd 2 *(Fig. 3a, page 2)*, join Dk Blue with slip st in any slip st; (ch 4, slip st in next slip st) around; ch 1, dc in first slip st to form last ch-4 sp.

Rnd 7: Ch 3 **(counts as first dc, now and throughout)**, 3 dc in same sp, 4 dc in next ch-4 sp and in each ch-4 sp around; join with slip st to first dc: 24 dc.

Rnd 8: Slip st in next dc, ch 3, dc in same st, ch 2, skip next dc, (2 dc in next dc, ch 2, skip next dc) around; join with slip st to first dc: 24 dc and 12 ch-2 sps.

Rnd 9: Ch 3, dc in same st, 2 dc in next dc, ch 2, dc in next dc, slip st in back ridge of sixth ch of next ch-12 on Rnd 5 *(Fig. 1, page 1)*, dc in next dc, ch 2, ★ 2 dc in each of next 2 dc, ch 2, dc in next dc, slip st in back ridge of sixth ch of next ch-12 on Rnd 5, dc in next dc, ch 2; repeat from ★ around; join with slip st to first dc: 36 dc and 12 ch-2 sps.

Rnd 10: Ch 2 **(counts as first hdc, now and throughout)**, hdc in next dc and in each dc and each ch-2 sp around; join with slip st to first hdc, finish off: 48 hdc.

Rnd 11: With **right** side facing and working in Back Loops Only, join Blue with slip st in same st as joining; work Beginning Cluster, ch 4, skip next 3 hdc, (work Cluster in next hdc, ch 4, skip next 3 hdc) twice, ★ (work Cluster, ch 4) twice in next hdc, skip next 3 hdc, (work Cluster in next hdc, ch 4, skip next 3 hdc) twice; repeat from ★ 2 times **more**, work Cluster in same st as Beginning Cluster, ch 4; join with slip st to top of Beginning Cluster: 16 Clusters and 16 ch-4 sps.

Rnd 12: Ch 3, ★ † (4 dc in next ch-4 sp, dc in next Cluster) 3 times, (2 dc, ch 2, 2 dc) in next corner ch-4 sp †, dc in next Cluster; repeat from ★ 2 times **more**, then repeat from † to † once; join with slip st to first dc: 80 dc and 4 ch-2 sps.

Rnd 13: Ch 2, ★ hdc in next dc and in each dc across to next corner ch-2 sp, (2 hdc, ch 2, 2 hdc) in corner ch-2 sp; repeat from ★ around to last 2 dc, hdc in last 2 dc; join with slip st to first hdc, finish off: 96 hdc and 4 ch-2 sps.

Square designed by Ann Lesage.

Finished Size: 8" square

MATERIALS
Worsted Weight Yarn - 56 yards
Crochet hook, size G (4.00 mm) **or** size needed for gauge

GAUGE SWATCH: 3" diameter
Work same as Square through Rnd 3.

STITCH GUIDE

TREBLE CROCHET *(abbreviated tr)*
YO twice, insert hook in st or sp indicated, YO and pull up a loop (4 loops on hook), (YO and draw through 2 loops on hook) 3 times.

PUFF STITCH *(abbreviated Puff St)*
★ YO, insert hook in sp indicated, YO and pull up a loop; repeat from ★ 2 times **more**, YO and draw through all 7 loops on hook.

DECREASE
Pull up a loop in same sp, skip next Puff St, pull up a loop in next sp, YO and draw through all 3 loops on hook **(counts as one sc)**.

Ch 4; join with slip st to form a ring.

Rnd 1 (Right side)**:** Ch 1, (work Puff St in ring, ch 2) 8 times; join with slip st to top of first Puff St: 8 Puff Sts and 8 ch-2 sps.

Note: Loop a short piece of yarn around any stitch to mark Rnd 1 as **right** side.

Rnd 2: Slip st in first ch-2 sp, ch 1, (work Puff St, ch 2) twice in same sp, work Puff St in next ch-2 sp, ch 2, ★ (work Puff St, ch 2) twice in next ch-2 sp, work Puff St in next ch-2 sp, ch 2; repeat from ★ 2 times **more**; join with slip st to top of first Puff St: 12 Puff Sts and 12 ch-2 sps.

Rnd 3: Slip st in first ch-2 sp, ch 1, (work Puff St, ch 2) twice in same sp, (work Puff St in next ch-2 sp, ch 2) twice, ★ (work Puff St, ch 2) twice in next ch-2 sp, (work Puff St in next ch-2 sp, ch 2) twice; repeat from ★ 2 times **more**; join with slip st to top of first Puff St: 16 Puff Sts and 16 ch-2 sps.

Rnd 4: Slip st in first ch-2 sp, ch 1, (work Puff St, ch 2) twice in same sp, (work Puff St in next ch-2 sp, ch 2) 3 times, ★ (work Puff St, ch 2) twice in next ch-2 sp, (work Puff St in next ch-2 sp, ch 2) 3 times; repeat from ★ 2 times **more**; join with slip st to top of first Puff St: 20 Puff Sts and 20 ch-2 sps.

Rnd 5: Slip st in first ch-2 sp, ch 3, 6 dc in same sp, ch 1, work Puff St in next ch-2 sp, (ch 2, work Puff St in next ch-2 sp) 3 times, ch 1, ★ 7 dc in next ch-2 sp, ch 1, work Puff St in next ch-2 sp, (ch 2, work Puff St in next ch-2 sp) 3 times, ch 1; repeat from ★ 2 times **more**; join with slip st to top of beginning ch-3: 44 sts and 20 sps.

Rnd 6: Ch 4 **(counts as first dc plus ch 1, now and throughout)**, (dc in next dc, ch 1) twice, (tr, ch 1) twice in next dc, dc in next dc, (ch 1, dc in next dc) twice, ch 2, skip next ch-1 sp, (work Puff St in next ch-2 sp, ch 2) 3 times, skip next Puff St, ★ (dc in next dc, ch 1) 3 times, (tr, ch 1) twice in next dc, dc in next dc, (ch 1, dc in next dc) twice, ch 2, skip next ch-1 sp, (work Puff St in next ch-2 sp, ch 2) 3 times, skip next Puff St; repeat from ★ 2 times **more**; join with slip st to first dc: 44 sts and 44 sps.

Rnd 7: Ch 4, (dc in next ch-1 sp, ch 1) 3 times, (tr, ch 1) twice in next ch-1 sp, (dc in next ch-1 sp, ch 1) 3 times, dc in next dc, ch 3, skip next ch-2 sp, work Puff St in next ch-2 sp, ch 2, work Puff St in next ch-2 sp, ch 3, skip next Puff St, ★ dc in next dc, ch 1, (dc in next ch-1 sp, ch 1) 3 times, (tr, ch 1) twice in next ch-1 sp, (dc in next ch-1 sp, ch 1) 3 times, dc in next dc, ch 3, skip next ch-2 sp, work Puff St in next ch-2 sp, ch 2, work Puff St in next ch-2 sp, ch 3, skip next Puff St; repeat from ★ 2 times **more**; join with slip st to first dc: 48 sts and 48 sps.

Rnd 8: Ch 4, (dc in next ch-1 sp, ch 1) 4 times, (tr, ch 1) twice in next ch-1 sp, (dc in next ch-1 sp, ch 1) 4 times, dc in next dc, ch 3, skip next ch-3 sp, work Puff St in next ch-2 sp, ch 3, skip next Puff St, ★ dc in next dc, ch 1, (dc in next ch-1 sp, ch 1) 4 times, (tr, ch 1) twice in next ch-1 sp, (dc in next ch-1 sp, ch 1) 4 times, dc in next dc, ch 3, skip next ch-3 sp, work Puff St in next ch-2 sp, ch 3, skip next Puff St; repeat from ★ 2 times **more**; join with slip st to first dc: 52 sts and 52 sps.

Rnd 9: Ch 1, sc in same st, ★ † (sc in next ch-1 sp and in next st) 5 times, 3 sc in next corner ch-1 sp, sc in next tr, (sc in next ch-1 sp and in next dc) 5 times, 3 sc in next ch-3 sp, decrease, 3 sc in same sp †, sc in next dc; repeat from ★ 2 times **more**, then repeat from † to † once; join with slip st to first sc, finish off: 128 sc.

Square designed by Nanette M. Seale.

13

Finished Size: 8" square

MATERIALS
Worsted Weight Yarn:
 Ecru - 27 yards
 Green - 8 yards
 Purple - 7 yards
 Yellow - 3 yards
Crochet hook, size H (5.00 mm) **or** size needed for gauge

GAUGE SWATCH: 3½" diameter
Work same as Square through Rnd 2.

STITCH GUIDE

TREBLE CROCHET (abbreviated tr)
YO twice, insert hook in sp indicated, YO and pull up a loop (4 loops on hook), (YO and draw through 2 loops on hook) 3 times.

BEGINNING CLUSTER (uses one sp)
Ch 3, ★ YO twice, insert hook in sp indicated, YO and pull up a loop, (YO and draw through 2 loops on hook) twice; repeat from ★ once **more**, YO and draw through all 3 loops on hook.

CLUSTER (uses one sp)
★ YO twice, insert hook in sp indicated, YO and pull up a loop, (YO and draw through 2 loops on hook) twice; repeat from ★ 2 times **more**, YO and draw through all 4 loops on hook.

With Yellow, ch 4; join with slip st to form a ring.

Rnd 1 (Right side)**:** Ch 5 **(counts as first dc plus ch 2, now and throughout)**, (dc in ring, ch 2) 7 times; join with slip st to first dc, finish off: 8 dc and 8 ch-2 sps.

Note: Loop a short piece of yarn around any stitch to mark Rnd 1 as **right** side.

Rnd 2: With **right** side facing, join Purple with slip st in any ch-2 sp; work Beginning Cluster in same sp, ch 4, (work Cluster in next ch-2 sp, ch 4) around; join with slip st to top of Beginning Cluster, finish off: 8 Clusters and 8 ch-4 sps.

Rnd 3: With **right** side facing, join Green with sc in any ch-4 sp *(see Joining With Sc, page 1)*; 5 sc in same sp, 6 sc in next ch-4 sp and in each ch-4 sp around; join with slip st to first sc, do **not** finish off: 48 sc.

Rnd 4: Ch 5, skip next sc, ★ dc in Back Loop Only of next sc *(Fig. 2, page 1)*, ch 2, skip next sc; repeat from ★ around; join with slip st to first dc, finish off: 24 dc and 24 ch-2 sps.

Rnd 5: With **right** side facing, join Ecru with sc in any ch-2 sp; ch 4, sc in next ch-2 sp, ch 3, sc in next ch-2 sp, ch 4, sc in next ch-2 sp, ch 5, sc in next ch-2 sp, ch 6, sc in next ch-2 sp, ★ ch 5, sc in next ch-2 sp, ch 4, sc in next ch-2 sp, ch 3, sc in next ch-2 sp, ch 4, sc in next ch-2 sp, ch 5, sc in next ch-2 sp, ch 6, sc in next ch-2 sp; repeat from ★ 2 times **more**, ch 2, dc in first sc to form last ch-5 sp; do **not** finish off.

Rnd 6: Ch 5, dc in next ch-4 sp, (ch 2, dc in next sp) 3 times, (ch 2, tr) 4 times in next ch-6 sp, ★ (ch 2, dc in next sp) 5 times, (ch 2, tr) 4 times in next ch-6 sp; repeat from ★ 2 times **more**, ch 1, sc in first dc to form last ch-2 sp: 36 sts and 36 ch-2 sps.

Rnd 7: Ch 3, dc in same sp, ch 1, (2 dc in next ch-2 sp, ch 1) 6 times, (2 dc, ch 3, 2 dc) in next corner ch-2 sp, ch 1, ★ (2 dc in next ch-2 sp, ch 1) 8 times, (2 dc, ch 3, 2 dc) in next corner ch-2 sp, ch 1; repeat from ★ 2 times **more**, ch 1, 2 dc in last ch-2 sp, ch 1; join with slip st to top of beginning ch-3, finish off: 80 dc and 40 sps.

Square designed by Martha Sadler.

14

Finished Size: 8" square

MATERIALS
Worsted Weight Yarn:
    Teal - 17 yards
    Purple - 15 yards
    Rose - 14 yards
    Lt Rose - 8 yards
    Lt Green - 8 yards
    Brown - 6 yards
Crochet hook, size I (5.50 mm) **or** size needed for gauge

GAUGE SWATCH: 2½" diameter
Work same as Square through Rnd 2.

STITCH GUIDE

TREBLE CROCHET *(abbreviated tr)*
YO twice, insert hook in st indicated, YO and pull up a loop (4 loops on hook), (YO and draw through 2 loops on hook) 3 times.

FRONT POST DOUBLE CROCHET *(abbreviated FPdc)*
YO, insert hook from **front** to **back** around post of st indicated *(Fig. 4, page 2)*, YO and pull up a loop (3 loops on hook), (YO and draw through 2 loops on hook) twice. Skip st behind FPdc.

With Brown, ch 6; join with slip st to form a ring.

Rnd 1 (Right side)**:** Ch 1, 12 sc in ring; join with slip st to first sc.

Note: Loop a short piece of yarn around any stitch to mark Rnd 1 as **right** side.

Rnd 2: Ch 3 **(counts as first dc, now and throughout)**, dc in same st, 2 dc in next sc and in each sc around; join with slip st to first dc, finish off: 24 dc.

Rnd 3: With **right** side facing, join Lt Rose with sc in any dc *(see Joining With Sc, page 1)*; work FPdc around next dc, (sc in next dc, work FPdc around next dc) around; join with slip st to first sc, do **not** finish off.

Rnd 4: Ch 3, dc in same st, work FPdc around next FPdc, (2 dc in next sc, work FPdc around next FPdc) around; join with slip st to first dc, finish off: 24 dc and 12 FPdc.

Rnd 5: With **right** side facing, join Lt Green with slip st in same st as joining; ch 4 **(counts as first dc plus ch 1, now and throughout)**, dc in next dc, work 2 FPdc around next FPdc, ★ dc in next dc, ch 1, dc in next dc, work 2 FPdc around next FPdc; repeat from ★ around; join with slip st to first dc, finish off: 24 dc, 24 FPdc, and 12 ch-1 sps.

Rnd 6: With **right** side facing, join Rose with slip st in first ch-1 sp; ch 4, dc in same sp, ch 1, (work FPdc around next FPdc, ch 1) twice, ★ (dc, ch 1) twice in next ch-1 sp, (work FPdc around next FPdc, ch 1) twice; repeat from ★ around; join with slip st to first dc, do **not** finish off: 24 dc, 24 FPdc, and 48 ch-1 sps.

Rnd 7: Slip st in first ch-1 sp, ch 1, sc in same sp and in next ch-1 sp, 3 sc in next ch-1 sp, (sc in next 3 ch-1 sps, 3 sc in next ch-1 sp) around to last ch-1 sp, sc in last ch-1 sp; join with slip st to first sc, finish off: 72 sc.

Rnd 8: With **right** side facing, join Teal with sc in same st as joining; hdc in next sc, dc in next sc, (tr, ch 3, tr) in next sc, dc in next sc, hdc in next sc, ★ sc in next 13 sc, hdc in next sc, dc in next sc, (tr, ch 3, tr) in next sc, dc in next sc, hdc in next sc; repeat from ★ 2 times **more**, sc in last 12 sc; join with slip st to first sc, do **not** finish off: 76 sts and 4 ch-3 sps.

Rnd 9: Ch 3, dc in next hdc, hdc in next 2 sts, 5 sc in next corner ch-3 sp, hdc in next 2 sts, dc in next 2 sts, hdc in next 2 sc, sc in next 7 sc, hdc in next 2 sc, ★ dc in next 2 sts, hdc in next 2 sts, 5 sc in next corner ch-3 sp, hdc in next 2 sts, dc in next 2 sts, hdc in next 2 sc, sc in next 7 sc, hdc in next 2 sc; repeat from ★ 2 times **more**; join with slip st to first dc, finish off: 96 sts.

Rnd 10: With **right** side facing, join Purple with slip st in same st as joining; ch 3, ★ dc in next st and in each st across to center sc of next corner 5-sc group, (dc, ch 3, dc) in center sc; repeat from ★ 3 times **more**, dc in next sc and in each st across; join with slip st to first dc, finish off: 100 dc and 4 ch-3 sps.

Square designed by Colleen Gilbert.

15

Finished Size: 8" square

MATERIALS
Worsted Weight Yarn:
    Ecru - 29 yards
    Pink - 18 yards
    Green - 3 yards
Crochet hook, size H (5.00 mm) **or** size needed for gauge

GAUGE SWATCH: 2½" diameter
Work same as Square through Rnd 3.

STITCH GUIDE

FRONT POST DOUBLE CROCHET
  (abbreviated FPdc)
YO, insert hook from **front** to **back** around post of st indicated *(Fig. 4, page 2)*, YO and pull up a loop (3 loops on hook), (YO and draw through 2 loops on hook) twice. Skip st behind FPdc.

BEGINNING BOBBLE (uses one sp)
Ch 2, ★ YO, insert hook in sp indicated, YO and pull up a loop, YO and draw through 2 loops on hook; repeat from ★ once **more**, YO and draw through all 3 loops on hook.

BOBBLE (uses one sp)
★ YO, insert hook in sp indicated, YO and pull up a loop, YO and draw through 2 loops on hook; repeat from ★ 2 times **more**, YO and draw through all 4 loops on hook.

CLUSTER (uses next 3 sts)
★ YO, insert hook in **next** st, YO and pull up a loop, YO and draw through 2 loops on hook; repeat from ★ 2 times **more**, YO and draw through all 4 loops on hook.

With Green, ch 4; join with slip st to form a ring.

Rnd 1 (Right side)**:** Ch 1, 8 sc in ring; join with slip st to first sc.

Note: Loop a short piece of yarn around any stitch to mark Rnd 1 as **right** side.

Rnd 2: Ch 1, 2 sc in same st and in each sc around; join with slip st to first sc, finish off: 16 sc.

Rnd 3: With **right** side facing and working in Back Loops Only *(Fig. 2, page 1)*, join Pink with slip st in any sc; ch 3 **(counts as first dc, now and throughout)**, dc in next sc, ch 2, dc in next sc, ch 1, dc in next sc, ch 2, ★ dc in next 2 sc, ch 2, dc in next sc, ch 1, dc in next sc, ch 2; repeat from ★ 2 times **more**; join with slip st to first dc: 16 dc and 12 sps.

Rnd 4: Ch 3, working in both loops, dc in next dc, ch 2, work FPdc around next dc, ch 1, work FPdc around next dc, ch 2, ★ dc in next 2 dc, ch 2, work FPdc around next dc, ch 1, work FPdc around next dc, ch 2; repeat from ★ 2 times **more**; join with slip st to first dc: 8 dc, 8 FPdc, and 12 sps.

Rnd 5: Ch 3, dc in next dc, ch 3, work FPdc around next FPdc, ch 2, work FPdc around next FPdc, ch 3, ★ dc in next 2 dc, ch 3, work FPdc around next FPdc, ch 2, work FPdc around next FPdc, ch 3; repeat from ★ 2 times **more**; join with slip st to first dc.

Rnd 6: Ch 3, dc in next dc, ch 4, work FPdc around next FPdc, ch 3, work FPdc around next FPdc, ch 4, ★ dc in next 2 dc, ch 4, work FPdc around next FPdc, ch 3, work FPdc around next FPdc, ch 4; repeat from ★ 2 times **more**; join with slip st to first dc.

Rnd 7: Ch 1, sc in same st and in next dc, ch 5, work FPdc around next FPdc, ch 4, work FPdc around next FPdc, ch 5, ★ sc in next 2 dc, ch 5, work FPdc around next FPdc, ch 4, work FPdc around next FPdc, ch 5; repeat from ★ 2 times **more**; join with slip st to first sc.

Rnd 8: Ch 2, hdc in next sc, 3 hdc in next ch-5 sp, work FPdc around next FPdc, ch 5, work FPdc around next FPdc, 3 hdc in next ch-5 sp, ★ hdc in next 2 sc, 3 hdc in next ch-5 sp, work FPdc around next FPdc, ch 5, work FPdc around next FPdc, 3 hdc in next ch-5 sp; repeat from ★ 2 times **more**; join with slip st to top of beginning ch-2, finish off: 40 sts and 4 ch-5 sps.

Rnd 9: With **right** side facing, join Ecru with slip st in any ch-5 sp; work (Beginning Bobble, ch 4, Bobble) in same sp, ch 4, skip next FPdc, ★ (work Cluster, ch 4) 3 times, (work Bobble, ch 4) twice in next ch-5 sp, skip next FPdc; repeat from ★ 2 times **more**, work Cluster, (ch 4, work Cluster) twice, ch 2, hdc in top of Beginning Bobble to form last ch-4 sp: 20 sts and 20 ch-4 sps.

Rnd 10: Work Beginning Bobble in same sp, ch 4, (work Bobble, ch 4) twice in next corner ch-4 sp, ★ (work Bobble in next ch-4 sp, ch 4) 4 times, (work Bobble, ch 4) twice in next corner ch-4 sp; repeat from ★ 2 times **more**, (work Bobble in next ch-4 sp, ch 4) 3 times; join with slip st to top of Beginning Bobble: 24 Bobbles and 24 ch-4 sps.

Rnd 11: Ch 1, sc in same st, 4 sc in next ch-4 sp, sc in next Bobble, 5 sc in next corner ch-4 sp, ★ sc in next Bobble, (4 sc in next ch-4 sp, sc in next Bobble) 5 times, 5 sc in next corner ch-4 sp; repeat from ★ 2 times **more**, (sc in next Bobble, 4 sc in next ch-4 sp) 4 times; join with slip st to first sc, finish off: 124 sc.

Square designed by Joan Briar.

Finished Size: 8¼" square

MATERIALS
Worsted Weight Yarn:
  Lt Green - 28 yards
  Ecru - 24 yards
  Green - 12 yards
Crochet hook, size G (4.00 mm) **or** size needed for gauge

GAUGE SWATCH: 3¼" diameter
Work same as Square through Rnd 3.

STITCH GUIDE

TREBLE CROCHET *(abbreviated tr)*
YO twice, insert hook in st or sp indicated, YO and pull up a loop (4 loops on hook), (YO and draw through 2 loops on hook) 3 times.

DOUBLE TREBLE CROCHET *(abbreviated dtr)*
YO 3 times, insert hook in st indicated, YO and pull up a loop (5 loops on hook), (YO and draw through 2 loops on hook) 4 times.

With Lt Green, ch 5; join with slip st to form a ring.

Rnd 1 (Right side)**:** Ch 1, 12 sc in ring; join with slip st to first sc.

Note: Loop a short piece of yarn around any stitch to mark Rnd 1 as **right** side.

Rnd 2: Ch 1, sc in same st, dtr in next sc, (sc in next sc pushing dtr to **right** side, dtr in next sc) around; join with slip st to first sc pushing last dtr made to **right** side, finish off.

Rnd 3: With **right** side facing, join Green with slip st in any sc; ch 3 **(counts as first dc, now and throughout)**, (2 dc, ch 1, 3 dc) in same st, ch 1, (3 dc, ch 1) twice in next sc and in each sc around; join with slip st to first dc, finish off: 36 dc and 12 ch-1 sps.

Rnd 4: With **right** side facing, join Lt Green with slip st in any ch 1 sp; ch 3, 2 dc in same sp, ch 1, (3 dc in next ch-1 sp, ch 1) around; join with slip st to first dc, finish off.

Rnd 5: With **right** side facing, join Green with slip st in any ch-1 sp; ch 3, 2 dc in same sp, ch 2, (3 dc in next ch-1 sp, ch 2) around; join with slip st to first dc, finish off.

Rnd 6: With **right** side facing, join Lt Green with slip st in any ch-2 sp; ch 3, (dc, ch 1, 2 dc) in same sp, ch 1, (2 dc, ch 1) twice in next ch-2 sp and in each ch-2 sp around; join with slip st to first dc, finish off: 48 dc and 24 ch-1 sps.

Rnd 7: With **right** side facing, join Ecru with slip st in first ch-1 sp; ch 4, ★ † tr in next dc, dc in next dc, dc in next ch-1 sp and in next 2 dc, hdc in next ch-1 sp, sc in next 2 dc, sc in next ch-1 sp and in next 2 dc, hdc in next ch-1 sp, dc in next 2 dc, dc in next ch-1 sp and in next dc, tr in next dc †, (tr, ch 2, tr) in next ch-1 sp; repeat from ★ 2 times **more**, then repeat from † to † once, tr in same sp as beginning ch-4, ch 2; join with slip st to top of beginning ch-4, do **not** finish off: 76 sts and 4 ch-2 sps.

Rnd 8: Ch 4, dc in next tr and in each st across to within one tr of next corner ch-2 sp, tr in next tr, (2 tr, ch 2, 2 tr) in corner ch-2 sp, ★ tr in next tr, dc in next tr and in each st across to within one tr of next corner ch-2 sp, tr in next tr, (2 tr, ch 2, 2 tr) in corner ch-2 sp; repeat from ★ 2 times **more**; join with slip st to top of beginning ch-4, finish off: 92 sts and 4 ch-2 sps.

Square designed by Janet Molik.

17

Finished Size: 8½" square

MATERIALS
Worsted Weight Yarn:
  White - 39 yards
  Purple - 27 yards
Crochet hook, size I (5.50 mm) **or** size needed
  for gauge

GAUGE SWATCH: 2½" diameter
Work same as Square through Rnd 2.

STITCH GUIDE

TREBLE CROCHET *(abbreviated tr)*
YO twice, insert hook in st indicated, YO and pull up a loop (4 loops on hook), (YO and draw through 2 loops on hook) 3 times.

FRONT POST DOUBLE CROCHET
  (abbreviated FPdc)
YO, insert hook from **front** to **back** around post of st indicated *(Fig. 4, page 2)*, YO and pull up a loop (3 loops on hook), (YO and draw through 2 loops on hook) twice. Skip st behind FPdc.

With Purple, ch 6; join with slip st to form a ring.

Rnd 1 (Right side)**:** Ch 1, 12 sc in ring; join with slip st to first sc.

Note: Loop a short piece of yarn around any stitch to mark Rnd 1 as **right** side.

Rnd 2: Ch 3 **(counts as first dc, now and throughout)**, dc in same st, 2 dc in next sc and in each sc around; join with slip st to first dc, finish off: 24 dc.

Rnd 3: With **right** side facing, join White with sc in any dc *(see Joining With Sc, page 1)*; work FPdc around next dc, (sc in next dc, work FPdc around next dc) around; join with slip st to first sc.

Rnd 4: Ch 3, dc in same st, work FPdc around next FPdc, (2 dc in next sc, work FPdc around next FPdc) around; join with slip st to first dc: 24 dc and 12 FPdc.

Rnd 5: Ch 4 **(counts as first dc plus ch 1, now and throughout)**, dc in next dc, work 2 FPdc around next FPdc, ★ dc in next dc, ch 1, dc in next dc, work 2 FPdc around next FPdc; repeat from ★ around; join with slip st to first dc, finish off: 24 dc, 24 FPdc, and 12 ch-1 sps.

Rnd 6: With **right** side facing, join Purple with slip st in first ch-1 sp; ch 4, dc in same sp, ch 1, (work FPdc around next FPdc, ch 1) twice, ★ (dc, ch 1) twice in next ch-1 sp, (work FPdc around next FPdc, ch 1) twice; repeat from ★ around; join with slip st to first dc: 24 dc, 24 FPdc, and 48 ch-1 sps.

Rnd 7: Slip st in first ch-1 sp, ch 1, sc in same sp and in next ch-1 sp, 3 sc in next ch-1 sp, (sc in next 3 ch-1 sps, 3 sc in next ch-1 sp) around to last ch-1 sp, sc in last ch-1 sp; join with slip st to first sc: 72 sc.

Rnd 8: Ch 1, sc in same st, hdc in next sc, dc in next sc, (tr, ch 3, tr) in next sc, dc in next sc, hdc in next sc, ★ sc in next 13 sc, hdc in next sc, dc in next sc, (tr, ch 3, tr) in next sc, dc in next sc, hdc in next sc; repeat from ★ 2 times **more**, sc in last 12 sc; join with slip st to first sc, finish off: 76 sts and 4 ch-3 sps.

Rnd 9: With **right** side facing, join White with slip st in same st as joining; ch 3, dc in next hdc, hdc in next 2 sts, 5 sc in next corner ch-3 sp, hdc in next 2 sts, dc in next 2 sts, hdc in next 2 sc, sc in next 7 sc, hdc in next 2 sc, ★ dc in next 2 sts, hdc in next 2 sts, 5 sc in next corner ch-3 sp, hdc in next 2 sts, dc in next 2 sts, hdc in next 2 sc, sc in next 7 sc, hdc in next 2 sc; repeat from ★ 2 times **more**; join with slip st to first dc: 96 sts.

Rnd 10: Ch 3, ★ dc in next st and in each st across to center sc of next corner 5-sc group, (dc, ch 3, dc) in center sc; repeat from ★ 3 times **more**, dc in next sc and in each st across; join with slip st to first dc, finish off: 100 dc and 4 ch-3 sps.

Square designed by Colleen Gilbert.

18

Finished Size: 8" square

MATERIALS
Worsted Weight Yarn:
   Purple - 53 yards
   Red - 18 yards
Crochet hook, size E (3.50 mm) **or** size needed for gauge

GAUGE SWATCH: 2" diameter
Work same as Square through Rnd 3.

STITCH GUIDE

SINGLE CROCHET POPCORN
(abbreviated sc Popcorn)
5 Sc in sc indicated, drop loop from hook, insert hook from **back** to **front** in first sc of 5-sc group, hook dropped loop and draw through.

BEGINNING DOUBLE CROCHET POPCORN
(abbreviated Beginning dc Popcorn)
Ch 3 **(counts as first dc)**, 4 dc in same st, drop loop from hook, insert hook from **back** to **front** in first dc of 5-dc group, hook dropped loop and draw through.

DOUBLE CROCHET POPCORN
(abbreviated dc Popcorn)
5 Dc in sc indicated, drop loop from hook, insert hook from **back** to **front** in first dc of 5-dc group, hook dropped loop and draw through.

With Red, ch 4; join with slip st to form a ring.

Rnd 1 (Right side)**:** Ch 1, 10 sc in ring; join with slip st to first sc.

Note: Loop a short piece of yarn around any stitch to mark Rnd 1 as **right** side.

Rnd 2: Ch 1, 2 sc in same st and in each sc around; join with slip st to first sc: 20 sc.

Rnd 3: Ch 1, **turn**; work sc Popcorn in same st, ch 2, skip next sc, ★ work sc Popcorn in next sc, ch 2, skip next sc; repeat from ★ around; join with slip st to first sc Popcorn, finish off: 10 sc Popcorns and 10 ch-2 sps.

Rnd 4: With **wrong** side facing, join Purple with sc in any ch-2 sp *(see Joining With Sc, page 1)*; sc in same sp, ch 1, (2 sc in next ch-2 sp, ch 1) around; join with slip st to first sc: 20 sc and 10 ch-1 sps.

Rnd 5: Ch 3 **(counts as first dc, now and throughout)**, turn; 2 dc in next ch-1 sp, (dc in next 2 sc, 2 dc in next ch-1 sp) around to last sc, dc in last sc; join with slip st to first dc: 40 dc.

Rnd 6: Ch 1, turn; sc in same st and in each dc around; join with slip st to first sc, finish off.

Rnd 7: With **wrong** side facing, join Red with slip st in same st as joining; work Beginning dc Popcorn, ch 2, skip next sc, ★ work dc Popcorn in next sc, ch 2, skip next sc; repeat from ★ around; join with slip st to top of Beginning dc Popcorn, finish off: 20 dc Popcorns and 20 ch-2 sps.

Rnd 8: With **wrong** side facing, join Purple with sc in any ch-2 sp; sc in same sp, sc in next dc Popcorn, (2 sc in next ch-2 sp, sc in next dc Popcorn) around; join with slip st to first sc: 60 sc.

Rnd 9: Ch 3, turn; dc in same st and in next 2 sc, (2 dc in next sc, dc in next 2 sc) around; join with slip st to first dc: 80 dc.

Rnd 10: Ch 1, do **not** turn; sc in same st, ★ ch 2, skip next dc, sc in next dc; repeat from ★ around to last dc, ch 1, sc in first sc to form last ch-2 sp: 40 ch-2 sps.

Rnd 11: Ch 1, sc in same sp, ★ † (ch 3, sc in next ch-2 sp) 6 times, ch 4, skip next ch-2 sp, (dc, ch 4) twice in next ch-2 sp, skip next ch-2 sp †, sc in next ch-2 sp; repeat from ★ 2 times **more**, then repeat from † to † once; join with slip st to first sc: 36 sps.

Rnd 12: Slip st in first ch-3 sp, ch 3, 2 dc in same sp, 3 dc in each of next 5 ch-3 sps, 4 dc in next ch-4 sp, ch 2, (dc, ch 2) 3 times in next corner ch-4 sp, 4 dc in next ch-4 sp, ★ 3 dc in each of next 6 ch-3 sps, 4 dc in next ch-4 sp, ch 2, (dc, ch 2) 3 times in next corner ch-4 sp, 4 dc in next ch-4 sp; repeat from ★ 2 times **more**; join with slip st to first dc: 116 dc and 16 ch-2 sps.

Rnd 13: Ch 1, sc in same st and in each dc across to next ch-2 sp, ch 3, (sc in next dc, ch 3) 3 times, ★ sc in next dc and in each dc across to next ch-2 sp, ch 3, (sc in next dc, ch 3) 3 times; repeat from ★ 2 times **more**, sc in last 4 dc; join with slip st to first sc.

Rnd 14: Ch 1, sc in same st and in each sc across to next ch-3 sp, ch 4, (sc in next sc, ch 4) 3 times, ★ sc in next sc and in each sc across to next ch-3 sp, ch 4, (sc in next sc, ch 4) 3 times; repeat from ★ 2 times **more**, sc in last 4 sc; join with slip st to first sc, finish off.

Square designed by Valarie Vandegriff.

19

Finished Size: 8¼" square

MATERIALS
Worsted Weight Yarn:
  Blue - 40 yards
  White - 20 yards
  Lt Blue - 17 yards
Crochet hook, size H (5.00 mm) **or** size needed for gauge

GAUGE SWATCH: 2" square
Work same as Center through Rnd 2.

STITCH GUIDE

TREBLE CROCHET *(abbreviated tr)*
YO twice, insert hook in sp indicated, YO and pull up a loop (4 loops on hook), (YO and draw through 2 loops on hook) 3 times.

BEGINNING DECREASE
Pull up a loop in first 2 sc, YO and draw through all 3 loops on hook **(counts as one sc)**.

ENDING DECREASE
Pull up a loop in last 2 sc, YO and draw through all 3 loops on hook **(counts as one sc)**.

CENTER

With Blue, ch 4; join with slip st to form a ring.

Rnd 1 (Right side): Ch 3 **(counts as first dc, now and throughout)**, (dc, tr) in ring, (2 dc, tr) 3 times in ring; join with slip st to first dc: 12 sts.

Note: Loop a short piece of yarn around any stitch to mark Rnd 1 as **right** side.

Rnd 2: Ch 3, dc in next dc, 5 dc in next tr, (dc in next 2 dc, 5 dc in next tr) around; join with slip st to first dc, finish off: 28 dc.

Rnd 3: With **right** side facing, join Lt Blue with slip st in center dc of any corner 5-dc group; ch 3, 4 dc in same st, dc in next 6 dc, (5 dc in next dc, dc in next 6 dc) around; join with slip st to first dc, finish off: 44 dc.

Rnd 4: With **right** side facing, join White with slip st in center dc of any corner 5-dc group; ch 3, 4 dc in same st, dc in next 10 dc, (5 dc in next dc, dc in next 10 dc) around; join with slip st to first dc, finish off: 60 dc.

FIRST POINT
Row 1: With **right** side facing, join Blue with sc in center dc of any corner 5-dc group *(see Joining With Sc, page 1)*; sc in next 15 dc, leave remaining dc unworked: 16 sc.

Rows 2-7: Ch 1, turn; work beginning decrease, sc in next sc and in each sc across to last 2 sc, work ending decrease: 4 sc.

Row 8: Ch 1, turn; work beginning decrease, work ending decrease: 2 sc.

Row 9: Ch 1, turn; work beginning decrease; finish off: one sc.

SECOND & THIRD POINTS
Row 1: With **right** side facing, join Blue with sc in same st as last sc on Row 1 of previous point; sc in next 15 dc, leave remaining dc unworked: 16 sc.

Rows 2-9: Work same as First Point: one sc.

FOURTH POINT
Row 1: With **right** side facing, join Blue with sc in same st as last sc on Row 1 of previous point; sc in next 14 dc and in same st as first sc on Row 1 of First Point: 16 sc.

Rows 2-8: Work same as First Point: 2 sc.

Row 9: Ch 1, turn; work beginning decrease; do **not** finish off: one sc.

BORDER
Rnd 1: Ch 1, do **not** turn; ★ working in end of rows and in sts at points, sc in first 9 rows, hdc in dc one row **below** (between points), sc in next 9 rows, 3 sc in next sc; repeat from ★ around; join with slip st to first sc, finish off: 88 sts.

Rnd 2: With **right** side facing, join Lt Blue with slip st in center sc of any corner 3-sc group; ch 3, 4 dc in same st, dc in next sc and in each st across to center sc of next corner 3-sc group, (5 dc in center sc, dc in next sc and in each st across to center sc of next corner 3-sc group) around; join with slip st to first dc, finish off: 104 dc.

Rnd 3: With **right** side facing, join White with sc in center dc of any corner 5-dc group; 4 sc in same st, sc in next dc and in each dc across to center dc of next corner 5-dc group, (5 sc in center dc, sc in next dc and in each dc across to center dc of next corner 5-dc group) around; join with slip st to first sc, finish off: 120 sc.

Square designed by Julene S. Watson.

20

Finished Size: 8" square

MATERIALS
Worsted Weight Yarn:
- White - 37 yards
- Red - 20 yards
- Blue - 19 yards

Crochet hook, size I (5.50 mm) **or** size needed for gauge

Yarn needle

GAUGE: 12 dc and 8 rows = $3^{3}/_{4}$"

Gauge Swatch: $1^{1}/_{4}$" square
Work same as Motif.

STITCH GUIDE

TREBLE CROCHET *(abbreviated tr)*
YO twice, insert hook in sp indicated, YO and pull up a loop (4 loops on hook), (YO and draw through 2 loops on hook) 3 times.

BLOCK (Make 2)
MOTIF

*Note: For **each** Block make 5 Motifs with Blue and make 4 Motifs with White.*

With color indicated, ch 4; join with slip st to form a ring.

Rnd 1 (Right side)**:** Ch 3 **(counts as first dc, now and throughout)**, (dc, tr) in ring, (2 dc, tr) 3 times in ring; join with slip st to first dc, finish off: 12 sts.

Note: Loop a short piece of yarn around any stitch to mark Rnd 1 as **right** side.

BLOCK ASSEMBLY
With White and working through **inside** loops only, whipstitch Motifs together and forming 2 vertical strips of 2 Blue Motifs and one White Motif and one vertical strip of 2 White Motifs and one Blue Motif *(Fig. 5b, page 2)*, beginning in first corner tr and ending in next corner tr. Placing Blue Motifs in corners, whipstitch 3 strips together in same manner to form Block.

STRIPES
FIRST SIDE
Row 1: With **right** side of Block facing, join Red with slip st in any corner tr; ch 3, dc in next 2 dc, (dc in same tr as joining on same Motif and in same tr as joining on next Motif, dc in next 2 dc) twice, dc in next tr, leave remaining sts unworked: 12 dc.

Row 2: Ch 3, turn; dc in next dc and in each dc across; finish off.

Row 3: With **right** side facing, join White with slip st in first dc; ch 3, dc in next dc and in each dc across.

Row 4: Ch 3, turn; dc in next dc and in each dc across; finish off.

Rows 5 and 6: With Red, repeat Rows 3 and 4.

Rows 7 and 8: Repeat Rows 3 and 4.

SECOND SIDE
Row 1: With **right** side of Block facing, join Red with slip st in same st as last dc on Row 1 of First Side; ch 3, dc in next 2 dc, (dc in same tr as joining on same Motif and in same tr as joining on next Motif, dc in next 2 dc) twice, dc in next tr, leave remaining sts unworked: 12 dc.

Rows 2-8: Work same as First Side.

SQUARE ASSEMBLY
With White and using photo as a guide, sew second Block to end of rows of First Side Stripes and Second Side Stripes.

BORDER
With **right** side facing, join Red with sc in any corner st *(see Joining With Sc, page 1)*; 2 sc in same st, work 22 sc evenly spaced across each side working 3 sc in each corner st; join with slip st to first sc, finish off: 100 sc.

Square designed by Julene S. Watson.

Finished Size: 7¾" square

MATERIALS
Worsted Weight Yarn:
 Black - 35 yards
 Red - 33 yards
Crochet hook, size H (5.00 mm) **or** size needed for gauge
Yarn needle

GAUGE SWATCH: 2½" square
Work same as Center through Rnd 2.

STITCH GUIDE

TREBLE CROCHET *(abbreviated tr)*
YO twice, insert hook in sp indicated, YO and pull up a loop (4 loops on hook), (YO and draw through 2 loops on hook) 3 times.

BEGINNING DECREASE
Pull up a loop in first 2 sts, YO and draw through all 3 loops on hook **(counts as one sc)**.

ENDING DECREASE
Pull up a loop in last 2 sts, YO and draw through all 3 loops on hook **(counts as one sc)**.

BLOCK A (Make 2)
CENTER
With Red, ch 4; join with slip st to form a ring.

Rnd 1 (Right side)**:** Ch 3 **(counts as first dc, now and throughout)**, (dc, tr) in ring, (2 dc, tr) 3 times in ring; join with slip st to first dc: 12 sts.

Note: Loop a short piece of yarn around any stitch to mark Rnd 1 as **right** side.

Rnd 2: Ch 3, dc in next dc, 5 dc in next tr, (dc in next 2 dc, 5 dc in next tr) 3 times; join with slip st to first dc: 28 dc.

Rnd 3: Ch 1, sc in same st and in next 3 dc, 3 sc in next dc, (sc in next 6 dc, 3 sc in next dc) 3 times, sc in last 2 dc; join with slip st to first sc, finish off: 36 sc.

FIRST POINT
Row 1: With **right** side facing, join Black with slip st in center sc of any corner 3-sc group; ch 1, pull up a loop in same st and in next sc, YO and draw through all 3 loops on hook, sc in next 6 sc, pull up a loop in next 2 sc, YO and draw through all 3 loops on hook, leave remaining sc unworked: 8 sts.

Rows 2 and 3: Ch 1, turn; work beginning decrease, sc in next sc and in each sc across to last 2 sc, work ending decrease: 4 sc.

Row 4: Ch 1, turn; work beginning decrease, work ending decrease: 2 sts.

Row 5: Ch 1, turn; work beginning decrease; finish off: one sc.

SECOND & THIRD POINTS
Row 1: With **right** side facing, join Black with slip st in same st as last sc on Row 1 of previous point; ch 1, pull up a loop in same st and in next sc, YO and draw through all 3 loops on hook, sc in next 6 sc, pull up a loop in next 2 sc, YO and draw through all 3 loops on hook, leave remaining sc unworked: 8 sts.

Rows 2-5: Work same as First Point: one sc.

FOURTH POINT
Row 1: With **right** side facing, join Black with slip st in same st as last sc on Row 1 of previous point; ch 1, pull up a loop in same st and in next sc, YO and draw through all 3 loops on hook, sc in next 6 sc, pull up a loop in next sc and in same st as first sc on Row 1 of First Point, YO and draw through all 3 loops on hook: 8 sts.

Rows 2-5: Work same as First Point: one sc.

BLOCK B (Make 2)
CENTER
With Black, work same as Block A.

POINTS
With Red, work same as Block A.

ASSEMBLY
With Black, using photo as a guide, and alternating Blocks, sew Blocks together forming 2 vertical strips of 2 Blocks each, then sew strips together.

Square designed by Julene S. Watson.

22

Finished Size: 8" square

MATERIALS
Worsted Weight Yarn - 52 yards
Crochet hook, size D (3.25 mm) **or** size needed for gauge

GAUGE SWATCH: 3¼" diameter
Work same as Square through Rnd 3.

STITCH GUIDE

TREBLE CROCHET *(abbreviated tr)*
YO twice, insert hook in st or sp indicated, YO and pull up a loop (4 loops on hook), (YO and draw through 2 loops on hook) 3 times.

PICOT
Ch 4, sc in fourth ch from hook.

SMALL PICOT LOOP
Ch 4, sc in third ch from hook, ch 1.

LARGE PICOT LOOP
Ch 5, sc in third ch from hook, ch 2.

Ch 5; join with slip st to form a ring.

Rnd 1 (Right side): Ch 4, (dc in ring, ch 1) 7 times; join with slip st to third ch of beginning ch-4: 8 sts and 8 ch-1 sps.

Note: Loop a short piece of yarn around any stitch to mark Rnd 1 as **right** side.

Rnd 2: Ch 1, sc in same st and in next ch-1 sp, work Picot, (sc in next dc and in next ch-1 sp, work Picot) around; join with slip st to first sc: 16 sc and 8 Picots.

Rnd 3: Slip st in next sc, ch 1, sc in same st, ★ ch 8, skip next Picot and next sc, sc in next sc; repeat from ★ around to last Picot, ch 4, skip last Picot and last sc, tr in first sc to form last ch-8 sp: 8 sc and 8 ch-8 sps.

Rnd 4: Ch 1, sc in same sp, ch 6, (sc in next ch-8 sp, ch 6) around; join with slip st to first sc.

Rnd 5: Ch 1, sc in same st, 6 sc in next ch-6 sp, (sc in next sc, 6 sc in next ch-6 sp) around; join with slip st to first sc: 56 sc.

Rnd 6: Ch 1, sc in same st and in each sc around; join with slip st to first sc.

Rnd 7: Ch 1, sc in same st, ★ ch 3, skip next sc, sc in next sc; repeat from ★ around to last sc, ch 1, skip last sc, hdc in first sc to form last ch-3 sp: 28 ch-3 sps.

Rnd 8: Ch 1, sc in same sp, (ch 5, sc in next ch-3 sp) around, ch 2, dc in first sc to form last ch-5 sp.

Rnd 9: Ch 1, sc in same sp, (ch 3, sc in next ch-5 sp) 5 times, (ch 2, tr) 4 times in next ch-5 sp, ★ ch 2, sc in next ch-5 sp, (ch 3, sc in next ch-5 sp) 5 times, (ch 2, tr) 4 times in next ch-5 sp; repeat from ★ 2 times **more**, ch 1, sc in first sc to form last ch-2 sp: 40 sts and 40 sps.

Rnd 10: Ch 1, sc in same sp, work Small Picot Loop, skip next sc, (sc in next sc, work Small Picot Loop) 4 times, skip next ch-3 sp, (sc in next ch-2 sp, work Large Picot Loop) 4 times, ★ sc in next ch-2 sp, work Small Picot Loop, skip next sc, (sc in next sc, work Small Picot Loop) 4 times, skip next ch-3 sp, (sc in next ch-2 sp, work Large Picot Loop) 4 times; repeat from ★ 2 times **more**; join with slip st to first sc: 36 sc and 36 Loops.

Rnd 11: Ch 1, sc in same st, (ch 5, skip next Loop, sc in next sc) 5 times, ★ (ch 8, skip next Loop, sc in next sc) 4 times, (ch 5, skip next Loop, sc in next sc) 5 times; repeat from ★ 2 times **more**, ch 8, skip next Loop, (sc in next sc, ch 8, skip next Loop) 3 times; join with slip st to first sc: 36 sps.

Rnd 12: Slip st in first ch-5 sp, ch 1, 3 sc in same sp and in each of next 4 ch-5 sps, 6 sc in each of next 4 ch-8 sps, (3 sc in each of next 5 ch-5 sps, 6 sc in each of next 4 ch-8 sps) 3 times; join with slip st to first sc, finish off: 156 sc.

Square designed by Valarie Vandegriff.

23

Finished Size: 8" square

MATERIALS
Worsted Weight Yarn:
  Ecru - 26 yards
  Green - 21 yards
Crochet hook, size E (3.50 mm) **or** size needed for gauge

GAUGE SWATCH: 2" square
Work same as Square through Rnd 2.

With Ecru, ch 5; join with slip st to form a ring.

Rnd 1 (Right side)**:** Ch 3 **(counts as first dc, now and throughout)**, 2 dc in ring, (ch 2, 3 dc in ring) 3 times, ch 1, sc in first dc to form last ch-2 sp: 12 dc and 4 ch-2 sps.

Note: Loop a short piece of yarn around any stitch to mark Rnd 1 as **right** side.

Rnd 2: Ch 1, 2 sc in same sp, sc in next 3 dc, ★ (2 sc, ch 2, 2 sc) in next ch-2 sp, sc in next 3 dc; repeat from ★ 2 times **more**, 2 sc in same sp as first sc, ch 1, sc in first sc to form last ch-2 sp: 28 sc and 4 ch-2 sps.

Rnd 3: Ch 1, working in Back Loops Only *(Fig. 2, page 1)*, 2 sc in same st, sc in next sc and in each sc across to next corner ch-2, 2 sc in next ch, ★ ch 2, 2 sc in next ch, sc in next sc and in each sc across to next corner ch-2, 2 sc in next ch; repeat from ★ 2 times **more**, ch 1, sc in **both** loops of first sc to form last ch-2 sp: 44 sc and 4 ch-2 sps.

Rnd 4: Ch 3, working in both loops, dc in next sc and in each sc across to next corner ch-2 sp, ★ (dc, ch 2, dc) in corner ch-2 sp, dc in each sc across to next corner ch-2 sp; repeat from ★ 2 times **more**, dc in same sp as first dc, ch 1, sc in first dc to form last ch-2 sp: 52 dc and 4 ch-2 sps.

Rnd 5: Ch 3, dc in next dc and in each dc across to next corner ch-2 sp, ★ (dc, ch 3, dc) in corner ch-2 sp, dc in each dc across to next corner ch-2 sp; repeat from ★ 2 times **more**, dc in same sp as first dc, ch 2, sc in first dc to form last ch-3 sp: 60 dc and 4 ch-3 sps.

Rnd 6: Ch 3, dc in next dc and in each dc across to next corner ch-3 sp, ★ (dc, ch 3, dc) in corner ch-3 sp, dc in each dc across to next corner ch-3 sp; repeat from ★ 2 times **more**, dc in same sp as first dc, ch 3; join with slip st to first dc, finish off: 68 dc and 4 ch-3 sps.

Rnd 7: With **right** side facing, join Green with sc in any corner ch-3 sp *(see Joining With Sc, page 1)*; 2 sc in same sp, sc in each dc across to next corner ch-3 sp, ★ 3 sc in corner ch-3 sp, sc in each dc across to next corner ch-3 sp; repeat from ★ 2 times **more**; join with slip st to first sc: 80 sc.

Rnd 8: Ch 1, sc in same st, ch 3, (sc in next sc, ch 3) twice, ★ (skip next sc, sc in next sc, ch 3) across to within one sc of next corner 3-sc group, skip next sc, (sc in next sc, ch 3) 3 times; repeat from ★ 2 times **more**, skip next sc, sc in next sc, (ch 3, skip next sc, sc in next sc) across to last sc, ch 1, skip last sc, hdc in first sc to form last ch-3 sp: 44 ch-3 sps.

Rnd 9: Ch 1, sc in same sp, (ch 4, sc in next ch-3 sp) around, ch 2, hdc in first sc to form last ch-4 sp.

Rnd 10: Ch 1, sc in same sp, ch 5, (sc in next ch-4 sp, ch 5) around; join with slip st to first sc, finish off.

INNER RUFFLE

Rnd 1: With **right** side facing, and working in free loops of sc on Rnd 2 *(Fig. 3a, page 2)*, join Green with sc in second ch of any corner ch-2; sc in same st and in next 7 sc, (2 sc in each of next 2 chs, sc in next 7 sc) 3 times, 2 sc in last ch; join with slip st to **both** loops of first sc: 44 sc.

Rnd 2: Ch 1, working in both loops, sc in same st, ★ ch 3, skip next sc, sc in next sc; repeat from ★ around to last sc, ch 1, skip last sc, hdc in first sc to form last ch-3 sp: 22 ch-3 sps.

Rnd 3: Ch 1, sc in same sp, ch 3, (sc in next ch-3 sp, ch 3) around; join with slip st to first sc, finish off.

Square designed by Valarie Vandegriff.

24

Finished Size: 8" square

MATERIALS
Worsted Weight Yarn:
  Teal - 22 yards
  Yellow - 19 yards
  Brown - 13 yards
Crochet hook, size H (5.00 mm) **or** size needed for gauge

GAUGE SWATCH: 3¾" diameter
Work same as Square through Rnd 3.

STITCH GUIDE

TREBLE CROCHET *(abbreviated tr)*
YO twice, insert hook in st indicated, YO and pull up a loop (4 loops on hook), (YO and draw through 2 loops on hook) 3 times.

DOUBLE TREBLE CROCHET *(abbreviated dtr)*
YO 3 times, insert hook in st indicated, YO and pull up a loop (5 loops on hook), (YO and draw through 2 loops on hook) 4 times.

POPCORN
4 Dc in st indicated, drop loop from hook, insert hook in first dc of 4-dc group, hook dropped loop and draw through, ch 1 to close.

With Brown, ch 4; join with slip st to form a ring.

Rnd 1 *(Right side)*: Ch 3 **(counts as first dc, now and throughout)**, 11 dc in ring; join with slip st to first dc: 12 dc.

Note: Loop a short piece of yarn around any stitch to mark Rnd 1 as **right** side.

Rnd 2: Ch 3, dc in same st, (dc, work Popcorn) in next dc, ★ 2 dc in next dc, (dc, work Popcorn) in next dc; repeat from ★ around; join with slip st to first dc: 18 dc and 6 Popcorns.

Rnd 3: Ch 3, dc in same st, work Popcorn in next dc, 2 dc in next dc, dc in closing ch of next Popcorn, ★ 2 dc in next dc, work Popcorn in next dc, 2 dc in next dc, dc in closing ch of next Popcorn; repeat from ★ around; join with slip st to first dc, finish off: 30 dc and 6 Popcorns.

Rnd 4: With **right** side facing, join Yellow with sc in dc to **right** of any Popcorn *(see Joining With Sc, page 1)*; sc in closing ch of next Popcorn, 2 sc in next dc, sc in next 2 dc, 2 sc in next dc, ★ sc in next dc and in closing ch of next Popcorn, 2 sc in next dc, sc in next 2 dc, 2 sc in next dc; repeat from ★ around; join with slip st to first sc: 48 sc.

Rnd 5: Ch 1, sc in same st and in next sc, slip st in next sc, ch 6 **loosely**, sc in second ch from hook and in next 4 chs, slip st in next sc, ★ sc in next 2 sc, slip st in next sc, ch 6 **loosely**, sc in second ch from hook and in next 4 chs, slip st in next sc; repeat from ★ around; join with slip st to first sc: 12 half petals.

Rnd 6: Slip st in next sc, ★ † ch 3, skip next slip st and next ch, working in free loops of ch *(Fig. 3b, page 2)*, dc in next ch, hdc in next ch, sc in next ch, slip st in next ch, skip next ch (at end of half petal), slip st in next sc, sc in next sc, hdc in next sc, dc in next sc, ch 3, skip next sc and next slip st †, slip st in next 2 sc; repeat from ★ 10 times **more**, then repeat from † to † once; join with slip st to same st as joining, finish off: 12 petals.

Rnd 7: With **right** side facing and working in Back Loops Only *(Fig. 2, page 1)*, join Teal with sc in first slip st at end of any petal; sc in next slip st, hdc in next sc, dc in next hdc, tr in next dc, skip next 2 ch-3 sps, tr in next dc, dc in next hdc, hdc in next sc, ★ sc in next 2 slip sts, hdc in next sc, dc in next hdc, tr in next dc, skip next 2 ch-3 sps, tr in next dc, dc in next hdc, hdc in next sc; repeat from ★ around; join with slip st to **both** loops of first sc: 96 sts.

Rnd 8: Ch 1, working in both loops, sc in same st and in next 9 sts, hdc in next 2 sts, dc in next 2 tr, tr in next 2 sts, 2 dtr in next sc, ch 3, 2 dtr in next sc, tr in next 2 sts, dc in next 2 tr, hdc in next 2 sts, ★ sc in next 10 sts, hdc in next 2 sts, dc in next 2 tr, tr in next 2 sts, 2 dtr in next sc, ch 3, 2 dtr in next sc, tr in next 2 sts, dc in next 2 tr, hdc in next 2 sts; repeat from ★ 2 times **more**; join with slip st to first sc, finish off: 104 sts.

Square designed by Laurie Halama.

25

Finished Size: 8" square

MATERIALS
Worsted Weight Yarn:
 White - 25 yards
 Blue - 20 yards
 Lt Blue - 20 yards
Crochet hook, size H (5.00 mm) **or** size needed for gauge

GAUGE SWATCH: 3" diameter
Work same as Square through Rnd 2.

STITCH GUIDE

BEGINNING DC CLUSTER (uses one sp)
Ch 2, ★ YO, insert hook in sp indicated, YO and pull up a loop, YO and draw through 2 loops on hook; repeat from ★ 2 times **more**, YO and draw through all 4 loops on hook.

DC CLUSTER (uses one sp)
★ YO, insert hook in sp indicated, YO and pull up a loop, YO and draw through 2 loops on hook; repeat from ★ 3 times **more**, YO and draw through all 5 loops on hook.

BEGINNING TR CLUSTER (uses one sp)
Ch 3, ★ YO twice, insert hook in **same** sp, YO and pull up a loop, (YO and draw through 2 loops on hook) twice; repeat from ★ 2 times **more**, YO and draw through all 4 loops on hook.

TR CLUSTER (uses one sp)
★ YO twice, insert hook in sp indicated, YO and pull up a loop, (YO and draw through 2 loops) twice; repeat from ★ 3 times **more**, YO and draw through all 5 loops on hook.

SPLIT CLUSTER (uses next 2 sps)
† YO twice, insert hook in **next** ch-2 sp, YO and pull up a loop, (YO and draw through 2 loops on hook) twice, ★ YO twice, insert hook in **same** sp, YO and pull up a loop, (YO and draw through 2 loops on hook) twice; repeat from ★ once **more** †, skip next FPdc, repeat from † to † once, YO and draw through all 7 loops on hook.

FRONT POST DOUBLE CROCHET (abbreviated FPdc)
YO, insert hook from **front** to **back** around post of st indicated **(Fig. 4, page 2)**, YO and pull up a loop (3 loops on hook), (YO and draw through 2 loops on hook) twice. Skip st behind FPdc.

FRONT POST TREBLE CROCHET (abbreviated FPtr)
YO twice, insert hook from **front** to **back** around post of st indicated **(Fig. 4, page 2)**, YO and pull up a loop (4 loops on hook), (YO and draw through 2 loops on hook) 3 times. Skip st behind FPtr.

With White, ch 6; join with slip st to form a ring.

Rnd 1 (Right side)**:** Work Beginning dc Cluster in ring, ch 5, (work dc Cluster in ring, ch 5) 3 times; join with slip st to top of Beginning dc Cluster, finish off: 4 dc Clusters and 4 ch-5 sps.

Note: Loop a short piece of yarn around any stitch to mark Rnd 1 as **right** side.

Rnd 2: With **right** side facing, join Blue with slip st in any ch-5 sp; work Beginning tr Cluster, ch 3, work FPdc around next dc Cluster, ch 3, ★ work tr Cluster in next ch-5 sp, ch 3, work FPdc around next dc Cluster, ch 3; repeat from ★ 2 times **more**; join with slip st to top of Beginning tr Cluster, finish off: 4 tr Clusters, 4 FPdc, and 8 ch-3 sps.

Rnd 3: With **right** side facing, join Lt Blue with slip st in first ch-3 sp; work Beginning tr Cluster, ch 3, work tr Cluster in next ch-3 sp, ch 3, work FPdc around next tr Cluster, ch 3, ★ (work tr Cluster in next ch-3 sp, ch 3) twice, work FPdc around next tr Cluster, ch 3; repeat from ★ 2 times **more**; join with slip st to top of Beginning tr Cluster, finish off: 8 tr Clusters, 4 FPdc, and 12 ch-3 sps.

Rnd 4: With **right** side facing, join White with slip st in first ch-3 sp; ch 3 **(counts as first dc, now and throughout)**, (2 dc, ch 3, 3 dc) in same sp, ★ † work FPtr around next tr Cluster, 3 dc in next ch-3 sp, work FPtr around next FPdc, 3 dc in next ch-3 sp, work FPtr around next tr Cluster †, (3 dc, ch 3, 3 dc) in next ch-3 sp; repeat from ★ 2 times **more**, then repeat from † to † once; join with slip st to first dc, finish off: 12 FPtr, 48 dc, and 4 ch-3 sps.

Rnd 5: With **right** side facing, join Blue with slip st in any corner ch-3 sp; work Beginning tr Cluster, ★ † ch 2, work FPdc around each of next 3 dc, ch 2, (skip next FPtr, work FPdc around each of next 3 dc, ch 2) 3 times †, work tr Cluster in next corner ch-3 sp; repeat from ★ 2 times **more**, then repeat from † to † once; join with slip st to top of Beginning tr Cluster, finish off: 4 tr Clusters, 48 FPdc, and 20 ch-2 sps.

Rnd 6: With **right** side facing, join Lt Blue with slip st in first ch-2 sp; work Beginning tr Cluster, ★ † (dc in next 3 FPdc, work tr Cluster in next ch-2 sp) 4 times, ch 2, work FPdc around next tr Cluster, ch 2 †, work tr Cluster in next ch-2 sp; repeat from ★ 2 times **more**, then repeat from † to † once; join with slip st to top of Beginning tr Cluster, finish off: 20 tr Clusters, 48 dc, 4 FPdc, and 8 ch-2 sps.

Rnd 7: With **right** side facing, skip first tr Cluster and join White with slip st in next dc; ch 3, dc in next 2 dc, work FPdc around next tr Cluster, ★ (dc in next 3 dc, work FPdc around next tr Cluster) across to next ch-2 sp, ch 4, work Split Cluster, ch 4, work FPdc around next tr Cluster; repeat from ★ around; join with slip st to first dc, finish off: 72 sts and 8 ch-4 sps.

Square designed by Kathleen M. Bowman.

Finished Size: 8" square

MATERIALS
   Worsted Weight Yarn:
      Blue - 30 yards
      Lt Blue - 23 yards
   Crochet hook, size F (3.75 mm) **or** size needed for gauge

GAUGE SWATCH: 3¼" diameter
Work same as Square through Rnd 4.

STITCH GUIDE

TREBLE CROCHET *(abbreviated tr)*
YO twice, insert hook in st indicated, YO and pull up a loop (4 loops on hook), (YO and draw through 2 loops on hook) 3 times.

With Blue, ch 4; join with slip st to form a ring.

Rnd 1 (Right side)**:** Ch 1, 8 sc in ring; join with slip st to first sc.

Note: Loop a short piece of yarn around any stitch to mark Rnd 1 as **right** side.

Rnd 2: Ch 1, 2 sc in same st and in each sc around; join with slip st to first sc: 16 sc.

Rnd 3: Ch 3 **(counts as first dc, now and throughout)**, dc in same st and in next 3 sc, ★ (2 dc, ch 1, 2 dc) in next sc, dc in next 3 sc; repeat from ★ 2 times **more**, 2 dc in same st as first dc, sc in first dc to form last ch-1 sp: 28 dc and 4 ch-1 sps.

Rnd 4: Ch 3, (dc, ch 2, 2 dc) in same sp, ch 4, skip next 3 dc, slip st in next dc, ch 4, skip next 3 dc, ★ (2 dc, ch 2, 2 dc) in next ch-1 sp, ch 4, skip next 3 dc, slip st in next dc, ch 4, skip next 3 dc; repeat from ★ 2 times **more**; join with slip st to first dc, finish off: 16 dc and 12 sps.

Rnd 5: With **right** side facing, join Lt Blue with slip st in any corner ch-2 sp; ch 3, dc in same sp, skip next 2 dc, dc in Back Loop Only of next 4 chs *(Fig. 2, page 1)*, tr in **both** loops of next slip st, dc in Back Loop Only of next 4 chs, skip next 2 dc, ★ (2 dc, ch 2, 2 dc) in next corner ch-2 sp, skip next 2 dc, dc in Back Loop Only of next 4 chs, tr in **both** loops of next slip st, dc in Back Loop Only of next 4 chs, skip next 2 dc; repeat from ★ 2 times **more**, 2 dc in same sp as first dc, ch 1, sc in first dc to form last ch-2 sp: 52 sts and 4 ch-2 sps.

Rnd 6: Ch 3, dc in same sp and in each st across to next corner ch-2 sp, ★ (2 dc, ch 2, 2 dc) in corner ch-2 sp, dc in each st across to next corner ch-2 sp; repeat from ★ 2 times **more**, 2 dc in same sp as first dc, ch 1, sc in first dc to form last ch-2 sp: 68 dc and 4 ch-2 sps.

Rnd 7: Ch 3, dc in same sp and in each dc across to next corner ch-2 sp, ★ (2 dc, ch 3, 2 dc) in corner ch-2 sp, dc in each st across to next corner ch-2 sp; repeat from ★ 2 times **more**, 2 dc in same sp as first dc, ch 3; join with slip st to first dc, finish off: 84 dc and 4 ch-3 sps.

Rnd 8: With **right** side facing, join Blue with slip st in any corner ch-3 sp; ch 3, dc in same sp and in each dc across to next corner ch-3 sp, ★ (2 dc, ch 2, 2 dc) in corner ch-3 sp, dc in each dc across to next corner ch-3 sp; repeat from ★ 2 times **more**, 2 dc in same sp as first dc, ch 2; join with slip st to first dc: 100 dc and 4 ch-2 sps.

Rnd 9: Ch 2, ★ hdc in next dc and in each dc across to next corner ch-2 sp, (hdc, ch 1, hdc) in corner ch-2 sp; repeat from ★ around; join with slip st to top of beginning ch-2, finish off: 108 sts and 4 ch-1 sps.

Square designed by Catherine Johnson.

27

Finished Size: 8" square

MATERIALS
Worsted Weight Yarn:
  Pink - 32 yards
  White - 20 yards
Crochet hook, size H (5.00 mm) **or** size needed for gauge

GAUGE SWATCH: 4"w x 4"h
Work same as Square through Rnd 4.

STITCH GUIDE

TREBLE CROCHET (*abbreviated tr*)
YO twice, insert hook in st or sp indicated, YO and pull up a loop (4 loops on hook), (YO and draw through 2 loops on hook) 3 times.

With Pink, ch 4; join with slip st to form a ring.

Rnd 1 (Right side)**:** Ch 1, 14 sc in ring; join with slip st to first sc.

Note: Loop a short piece of yarn around any stitch to mark Rnd 1 as **right** side.

Rnd 2: Ch 4, 2 tr in each of next 2 sc, 2 dc in each of next 2 sc, 2 hdc in each of next 2 sc, ch 1, tr in next sc, ch 1, 2 hdc in each of next 2 sc, 2 dc in each of next 2 sc, 2 tr in each of next 2 sc, ch 4, slip st in sc at base of beginning ch-4: 26 sts and 10 chs.

Rnd 3: Ch 1, working **around** first slip st, sc in same st as slip st, working in Back Loops Only *(Fig. 2, page 1)*, sc in next 4 chs, sc in next 12 sts and in next ch, 3 sc in next tr, sc in next ch, sc in next 12 sts and in next 4 chs; join with slip st to **both** loops of first sc: 38 sc.

Rnd 4: Working in both loops, slip st in next 2 sc, ch 1, sc in same st and in next 2 sc, 2 sc in each of next 6 sc, sc in next 8 sc, 3 sc in next sc, sc in next 8 sc, 2 sc in each of next 6 sc, sc in next 3 sc, leave remaining sts unworked; join with slip st to first sc, finish off: 49 sc.

Rnd 5: With **right** side facing, join White with sc in same st as joining; ★ ch 3, skip next sc, sc in next sc; repeat from ★ around; join with slip st to first sc: 25 sc and 24 ch-3 sps.

Rnd 6: Slip st in first ch-3 sp, ch 1, sc in same sp, (ch 3, sc in next ch-3 sp) around, dc in first sc to form last ch-3 sp.

Rnd 7: Ch 1, 3 sc in same sp, 3 hdc in next ch-3 sp, 3 dc in next ch-3 sp, (2 tr, ch 3, 2 tr) in next ch-3 sp, 3 dc in next ch-3 sp, 3 hdc in next ch-3 sp, 3 sc in next ch-3 sp, 3 dc in next ch-3 sp, 3 tr in next ch-3 sp, (2 tr, ch 3, 2 tr) in next ch-3 sp, 3 dc in next ch-3 sp, 3 sc in each of next 3 ch-3 sps, 3 dc in next ch-3 sp, (2 tr, ch 3, 2 tr) in next ch-3 sp, 3 tr in next ch-3 sp, 3 dc in next ch-3 sp, 3 sc in next ch-3 sp, 3 hdc in next ch-3 sp, 3 dc in next ch-3 sp, (2 tr, ch 3, 2 tr) in next ch-3 sp, 3 dc in next ch-3 sp, 3 hdc in last ch-3 sp; join with slip st to first sc, finish off: 76 sts and 4 ch-3 sps.

Rnd 8: With **right** side facing, join Pink with slip st in any corner ch-3 sp; ch 3, (dc, ch 3, 2 dc) in same sp, dc in each st across to next corner ch-3 sp, ★ (2 dc, ch 3, 2 dc) in corner ch-3 sp, dc in each st across to next corner ch-3 sp; repeat from ★ 2 times **more**; join with slip st to top of beginning ch-3: 92 sts and 4 ch-3 sps.

Rnd 9: Ch 1, sc in same st and in next dc, 3 sc in next corner ch-3 sp, (sc in each dc across to next corner ch-3 sp, 3 sc in corner ch-3 sp) 3 times, sc in each dc across; join with slip st to first sc, finish off: 104 sc.

Square designed by Colleen Gilbert.

28

Finished Size: 8½" square

MATERIALS
Worsted Weight Yarn - 72 yards
Crochet hook, size H (5.00 mm) **or** size needed for gauge

GAUGE SWATCH: 3¾" square
Work same as Square through Rnd 3.

STITCH GUIDE

FRONT POST TREBLE CROCHET
(abbreviated FPtr)
YO twice, insert hook from **front** to **back** around post of st indicated *(Fig. 4, page 2)*, YO and pull up a loop (4 loops on hook), (YO and draw through 2 loops on hook) 3 times. Skip st behind FPtr.

CROSS STITCH *(abbreviated Cross St)*
(uses next 2 dc)
Skip next dc, dc in next dc, working **behind** last dc made, dc in skipped dc.

Ch 3; join with slip st to form a ring.

Rnd 1 (Right side)**: Ch 3 (counts as first dc, now and throughout)**, 11 dc in ring; join with slip st to first dc: 12 dc.

Note: Loop a short piece of yarn around any stitch to mark Rnd 1 as **right** side.

Rnd 2: Ch 3, dc in next dc, (2 dc, ch 2, 2 dc) in next dc, ★ dc in next 2 dc, (2 dc, ch 2, 2 dc) in next dc; repeat from ★ 2 times **more**; join with slip st to first dc: 24 dc and 4 ch-2 sps.

Rnd 3: Ch 3, dc in next dc, work FPtr around each of next 2 dc, (2 dc, ch 2, 2 dc) in next corner ch-2 sp, work FPtr around each of next 2 dc, ★ dc in next 2 dc, work FPtr around each of next 2 dc, (2 dc, ch 2, 2 dc) in next corner ch-2 sp, work FPtr around each of next 2 dc; repeat from ★ 2 times **more**; join with slip st to first dc: 24 dc, 16 FPtr, and 4 ch-2 sps.

Rnd 4: Ch 3, dc in next dc, work FPtr around each of next 2 FPtr, dc in next 2 dc, (2 dc, ch 2, 2 dc) in next corner ch-2 sp, dc in next 2 dc, ★ (work FPtr around each of next 2 FPtr, dc in next 2 dc) twice, (2 dc, ch 2, 2 dc) in next corner ch-2 sp, dc in next 2 dc; repeat from ★ 2 times **more**, work FPtr around each of last 2 FPtr; join with slip st to first dc: 40 dc, 16 FPtr, and 4 ch-2 sps.

Rnd 5: Ch 3, dc in next dc, work FPtr around each of next 2 FPtr, dc in next 4 dc, (2 dc, ch 2, 2 dc) in next corner ch-2 sp, dc in next 4 dc, work FPtr around each of next 2 FPtr, ★ dc in next 2 dc, work FPtr around each of next 2 FPtr, dc in next 4 dc, (2 dc, ch 2, 2 dc) in next corner ch-2 sp, dc in next 4 dc, work FPtr around each of next 2 FPtr; repeat from ★ 2 times **more**; join with slip st to first dc: 56 dc, 16 FPtr, and 4 ch-2 sps.

Rnd 6: Ch 3, dc in next dc, work FPtr around each of next 2 FPtr, dc in next 6 dc, (2 dc, ch 2, 2 dc) in next corner ch-2 sp, dc in next 6 dc, work FPtr around each of next 2 FPtr, ★ dc in next 2 dc, work FPtr around each of next 2 FPtr, dc in next 6 dc, (2 dc, ch 2, 2 dc) in next corner ch-2 sp, dc in next 6 dc, work FPtr around each of next 2 FPtr; repeat from ★ 2 times **more**; join with slip st to first dc: 72 dc, 16 FPtr, and 4 ch-2 sps.

Rnd 7: Slip st in next dc, ch 3, working **behind** first dc made, dc in same st as joining, work FPtr around each of next 2 FPtr, work 4 Cross Sts, (2 dc, ch 2, 2 dc) in next corner ch-2 sp, work 4 Cross Sts, work FPtr around each of next 2 FPtr, ★ work Cross St, work FPtr around each of next 2 FPtr, work 4 Cross Sts, (2 dc, ch 2, 2 dc) in next corner ch-2 sp, work 4 Cross Sts, work FPtr around each of next 2 FPtr; repeat from ★ 2 times **more**; join with slip st to first dc: 88 dc, 16 FPtr, and 4 ch-2 sps.

Rnd 8: Ch 1, sc in same st and in each st around working 3 sc in each corner ch-2 sp; join with slip st to first sc, finish off: 116 sc.

Square designed by Roberta Maier.

40

29

Finished Size: 9¼"w x 10¼"h

MATERIALS
Worsted Weight Yarn:
　White - 67 yards
　Green - 30 yards
　Rose - 10 yards
Crochet hooks, sizes B (2.25 mm) **and** H (5.00 mm)
　or sizes needed for gauge
Safety pin
Yarn needle

GAUGE SWATCH: 3"w x 4"h
Work same as Motif through Rnd 3.

STITCH GUIDE

> **TREBLE CROCHET** *(abbreviated tr)*
> YO twice, insert hook in st indicated, YO and pull up a loop (4 loops on hook), (YO and draw through 2 loops on hook) 3 times.

MOTIF
With White and using large hook, ch 4; join with slip st to form a ring.

Rnd 1 (Right side)**:** Ch 1, 8 sc in ring; join with slip st to first sc.

Note: Loop a short piece of yarn around any stitch to mark Rnd 1 as **right** side.

Rnd 2: Ch 5, dc in same st, ch 2, (tr, ch 2) twice in next 2 sc, (dc, ch 2) twice in next 2 sc, (tr, ch 2) twice in next 2 sc, (dc, ch 2) twice in last sc; join with slip st to third ch of beginning ch-5: 16 sts and 16 ch-2 sps.

Rnd 3: Ch 1, sc in same st, 2 sc in next ch-2 sp, (sc in next st, 2 sc in next ch-2 sp) around; join with slip st to first sc: 48 sc.

Rnd 4: Ch 1, sc in same st, ch 1, skip next sc, (sc in next sc, ch 1, skip next sc) around; join with slip st to first sc, slip loop onto safety pin to keep piece from unraveling while working Rnd 5: 24 sc and 24 ch-1 sps.

Rnd 5: With **right** side facing and using large hook, join Rose with sc in Front Loop Only *(Fig. 2, page 1)* of same st as joining *(see Joining With Sc, page 1)*; working **behind** next ch-1, dc in skipped sc one rnd **below**, ★ sc in Front Loop Only of next sc, working **behind** next ch-1, dc in skipped sc one rnd **below**; repeat from ★ around; join with slip st to **both** loops of first sc, finish off: 48 sts.

Rnd 6: With **right** side facing, remove safety pin and slip loop onto large hook, ch 1, working **behind** Rnd 5 and in free loops of sc on Rnd 4 *(Fig. 3a, page 2)*, sc in same st as joining; ch 1, (sc in next sc, ch 1) around; join with slip st to first sc: 24 sc and 24 ch-1 sps.

Rnd 7: Ch 1, sc in same st and in next ch-1 sp, sc in next sc and in next ch-1 sp, † hdc in next sc, 2 dc in next ch-1 sp, (tr, ch 2, tr) in next sc, 2 dc in next ch-1 sp, hdc in next sc, sc in next ch-1 sp, (sc in next sc and in next ch-1 sp) twice, hdc in next sc, 2 dc in next ch-1 sp, (tr, ch 2, tr) in next sc, 2 dc in next ch-1 sp, hdc in next sc, sc in next ch-1 sp †, (sc in next sc and in next ch-1 sp) 4 times, repeat from † to † once, (sc in next sc and in next ch-1 sp) twice; join with slip st to first sc: 60 sts and 4 ch-2 sps.

Rnd 8: Ch 1, sc in same st and in each st across to next corner ch-2 sp, 3 sc in corner ch-2 sp, ★ sc in each st across to next corner ch-2 sp, 3 sc in corner ch-2 sp; repeat from ★ 2 times **more**, sc in each st across; join with slip st to first sc: 72 sc.

Rnd 9: Ch 1, **turn**; sc in same st, ★ (ch 1, skip next sc, sc in next sc) across to center sc of next corner 3-sc group, ch 3, skip center sc, sc in next sc; repeat from ★ 3 times **more**, ch 1, skip next sc, (sc in next sc, ch 1, skip next sc) across; join with slip st to first sc: 36 sc and 36 sps.

Rnd 10: Ch 1, do **not** turn; sc in same st, ch 1, ★ (sc in next sc, ch 1) across to next corner ch-3 sp, (sc, ch 3, sc) in corner ch-3 sp, ch 1; repeat from ★ 3 times **more**, (sc in next sc, ch 1) across; join with slip st to first sc, finish off: 44 sc and 44 sps.

Rnd 11: With **right** side facing and using large hook, join Green with sc in first sc to **right** of any corner ch-3 sp; ★ † working **behind** next corner ch-3, (dc, ch 3, dc) in ch-3 sp one rnd **below** (between sc), sc in next sc, working **behind** next ch-1, dc in same ch-3 sp one rnd **below** after last sc, sc in next sc, (working **behind** next ch-1, dc in ch-1 sp one rnd **below**, sc in next sc) across to within one ch-1 sp of next corner ch-3 sp, working **behind** next ch-1 sp, dc in next corner ch-3 sp **before** first sc †, sc in next sc; repeat from ★ 2 times **more**, then repeat from † to † once; join with slip st to first sc: 92 sts and 4 ch-3 sps.

Rnd 12: Ch 1, **turn**; sc in same st, ch 1, skip next dc, ★ (sc in next sc, ch 1, skip next dc) across to next corner ch-3 sp, (sc, ch 3, sc) in corner ch-3 sp, ch 1, skip next dc; repeat from ★ around; join with slip st to first sc, finish off: 52 sc and 52 sps.

41

Rnd 13: With **right** side facing and using large hook, join White with sc in first sc to **right** of any corner ch-3 sp; ★ † working **behind** next corner ch-3 sp, (dc, ch 1, dc) in corner ch-3 sp one rnd **below** (between sc), (sc in next sc, working **behind** next ch-1, dc in sp **before** dc one rnd **below**) across to within one sc of next corner ch-3 sp †, sc in next sc; repeat from ★ 2 times **more**, then repeat from † to † once; join with slip st to first sc: 108 sts and 4 ch-1 sps.

Rnd 14: Ch 3, **turn**; sc in next dc, ★ (dc in next sc, sc in next dc) across to next corner ch-1 sp, 3 sc in corner ch-1 sp, sc in next dc; repeat from ★ around; join with slip st to top of beginning ch-3: 120 sts.

Rnd 15: Ch 1, turn; sc in same st, dc in next sc, sc in next sc, 3 sc in next sc, ★ sc in next sc, (dc in next sc, sc in next st) across to center sc of next corner 3-sc group, 3 sc in center sc; repeat from ★ 2 times **more**, (sc in next st, dc in next sc) across; join with slip st to first sc, finish off: 128 sts.

Rnd 16: With **right** side facing and using large hook, join Green with sc in any st; sc in each st around working 3 sc in center sc of each corner 3-sc group; join with slip st to first sc, finish off: 136 sc.

FLOWER

Cut one 4-yard length of Rose and separate into two 2-ply lengths.

Using small hook and one 2-ply length, ch 24 **loosely**.

Row 1: Working in back ridge of beginning ch *(Fig. 1, page 1)*, dc in sixth ch from hook **(5 skipped chs count as first dc plus ch 2)**, (ch 2, dc in next ch) twice, ★ ch 2, skip next ch, dc in next ch; repeat from ★ across: 12 dc and 11 ch-2 sps.

Row 2 (Right side)**:** Ch 1, turn; (slip st, 4 dc, slip st) in first 5 ch-2 sps, (slip st, 3 dc, slip st) in next 4 ch-2 sps, (slip st, 2 dc, slip st) in last 2 ch-2 sps; finish off leaving a long end for sewing.

With **right** side facing and beginning at smaller end, roll Flower, securing base as you go.

LEAVES

Cut one 4-yard length of Green and separate into two 2-ply lengths.

Using small hook and one 2-ply length, ch 7; join with slip st to form a ring.

Rnd 1 (Right side)**:** Ch 1, 15 sc in ring; join with slip st to first sc.

Rnd 2: Ch 1, sc in same st, ch 5, (sc in next 5 sc, ch 5) twice, sc in last 4 sc; join with slip st to first sc: 15 sc and 3 ch-5 sps.

Rnd 3: ★ Slip st in first ch of next ch-5, ch 4, slip st in same ch and in next 2 chs, ch 6, slip st in same ch and in next 2 chs, ch 4, slip st in next 5 sc; repeat from ★ 2 times **more**; join with slip st to first slip st, finish off leaving a long end for sewing.

Thread yarn needle with yarn end and sew Flower to center of right side of Leaves, then sew Leaves to center of **right** side of Motif.

Motif designed by Thelma Moore.

30

Finished Size: 8" square

MATERIALS
Worsted Weight Yarn:
  White - 27 yards
  Black - 26 yards
Crochet hook, size H (5.00 mm) **or** size needed for gauge

GAUGE SWATCH: 4¼" diameter
Work same as Square through Rnd 3.

STITCH GUIDE

TREBLE CROCHET (abbreviated tr)
YO twice, insert hook in sp indicated, YO and pull up a loop (4 loops on hook), (YO and draw through 2 loops on hook) 3 times.

With Black, ch 6; join with slip st to form a ring.

Rnd 1 (Right side)**:** Ch 3 **(counts as first dc, now and throughout)**, 11 dc in ring; join with slip st to first dc, do **not** finish off: 12 dc.

Note #1: Loop a short piece of yarn around any stitch to mark Rnd 1 as **right** side.

Note #2: To **change colors**, work the last stitch to within one step of completion, hook new yarn, and draw through both loops on hook. Work **over** color not being used, holding it with normal tension. Do **not** cut yarn unless otherwise instructed.

Continued on page 43.

#30 Continued from page 42.

Rnd 2: Ch 3, working in Back Loops Only *(Fig. 2, page 1)*, dc in same st changing to White, ★ 2 dc in next dc changing to Black in last dc, 2 dc in next dc changing to White in last dc; repeat from ★ around to last dc, 2 dc in last dc, do **not** change colors; join with slip st to first dc: 24 dc.

Note: Continue to work in Back Loops Only and change colors in same manner.

Rnd 3: With White, ch 3, dc in same st, 2 dc in next dc, with Black 2 dc in each of next 2 dc, ★ with White 2 dc in each of next 2 dc, with Black 2 dc in each of next 2 dc; repeat from ★ around; with White, join with slip st to first dc, cut Black: 48 dc.

Rnd 4: Ch 1, sc in same st, ch 6, skip next 3 dc, ★ sc in next dc, ch 6, skip next 3 dc; repeat from ★ around; join with slip st to first sc: 12 sc and 12 ch-6 sps.

Rnd 5: Ch 1, (slip st in next 6 chs and in next sc) twice, (sc, hdc, dc, tr, dc, hdc, sc) in next ch-6 sp, ★ slip st in next sc, (slip st in next 6 chs and in next sc) twice, (sc, hdc, dc, tr, dc, hdc, sc) in next ch-6 sp; repeat from ★ 2 times **more**; join with slip st to beginning ch-1, finish off: 88 sts.

Rnd 6: With **right** side facing, join Black with sc in any corner tr *(see Joining With Sc, page 1)*; sc in next st and in each st around; join with slip st to first sc.

Rnd 7: Ch 1, sc in same st, ★ † ch 3, skip next sc, sc in next sc, ch 3, (skip next 2 sc, sc in next sc, ch 3) 6 times, skip next sc †, sc in next sc; repeat from ★ 2 times **more**, then repeat from † to † once; join with slip st to first sc, finish off: 32 ch-3 sps.

Rnd 8: With **right** side facing, join White with sc in first ch-3 sp; (ch 3, sc in next ch-3 sp) 7 times, ch 4, ★ sc in next ch-3 sp, (ch 3, sc in next ch-3 sp) 7 times, ch 4; repeat from ★ 2 times **more**; join with slip st to first sc.

Rnd 9: Slip st in first ch-3 sp, ch 3, 2 dc in same sp, ★ † (with Black 3 dc in next ch-3 sp, with White 3 dc in next ch-3 sp) 3 times, with Black (2 dc, 2 tr, 2 dc) in next ch-4 sp †, with White 3 dc in next ch-3 sp; repeat from ★ 2 times **more**, then repeat from † to † once, cut Black; join with slip st to first dc, finish off: 108 sts.

Square designed by Linda Tyler.

#1 Continued from page 3.

Rnd 2: Ch 4, **turn**; skip next sc, working in both loops, (dc in next sc, ch 1, skip next sc) across to center sc of next corner 3-sc group, ★ (dc, ch 1, tr, ch 1, dc) in center sc, ch 1, skip next sc, (dc in next sc, ch 1, skip next sc) across to center sc of next corner 3-sc group; repeat from ★ 2 times **more**, (dc, ch 1, tr) in same st as first dc, ch 1; join with slip st to first dc: 396 sts and 396 ch-1 sps.

Rnd 3: Ch 1, turn; sc in same st and in each ch and each dc around working 3 sc in each corner tr; join with slip st to first sc.

Rnd 4: Ch 1, do **not** turn; (slip st in next sc, ch 1) around; join with slip st to joining slip st, finish off.

Square designed by Laurie Halama.

#2 Continued from page 5.

ASSEMBLY

With Red, keeping top edges toward same end, and working through **both** loops, whipstitch Squares together forming 6 vertical strips of 8 Squares each *(Fig. 5a, page 2)*, beginning in center hdc of first corner 5-hdc group and ending in center hdc of next corner 5-hdc group; then whipstitch strips together in same manner.

EDGING

Rnd 1: With **right** side facing, join Red with sc in center hdc of any corner 5-hdc group; sc in same st and in each hdc and each joining across to center hdc of next corner 5-hdc group, ★ 3 sc in center hdc, sc in each hdc and in each joining across to center hdc of next corner 5-hdc group; repeat from ★ 2 times **more**, sc in same st as first sc; join with slip st to first sc: 708 sc.

Rnd 2: Ch 1, work (Puff St, ch 2, Puff St) in same st, ch 1, skip next sc, (work Puff St in next sc, ch 1, skip next sc) across to center sc of next corner 3-sc group, ★ work (Puff St, ch 2, Puff St) in center sc, ch 1, skip next sc, (work Puff St in next sc, ch 1, skip next sc) across to center sc of next corner 3-sc group; repeat from ★ 2 times **more**; join with slip st to first Puff St.

Rnd 3: Slip st in first ch-2 sp, ch 2, 4 hdc in same sp, ★ 2 hdc in each ch-1 sp across to next corner ch-2 sp, 5 hdc in corner ch-2 sp; repeat from ★ 2 times **more**, 2 hdc in each ch-1 sp across; join with slip st to first hdc, finish off.

Square designed by Nanette M. Seale.

#3 Continued from page 7.

ASSEMBLY

With Blue and working through **inside** loops only, whipstitch Squares together forming 6 vertical strips of 8 Squares each *(Fig. 5b, page 2)*, beginning in second ch of first corner ch-2 and ending in first ch of next corner ch-2; then whipstitch strips together in same manner.

EDGING

Rnd 1: With **right** side facing and working in Back Loops Only, join Ecru with sc in first ch of any corner ch-2; ch 2, sc in next ch, ★ sc in each sc and in each ch across to next corner ch-2, sc in next ch, ch 2, sc in next ch; repeat from ★ 2 times **more**, sc in each sc and in each ch across; join with slip st to **both** loops of first sc, finish off: 812 sc.

Rnd 2: With **right** side facing, join Blue with sc in any corner ch-2 sp; ch 2, sc in same sp, working in both loops, sc in each sc across to next corner ch-2 sp, ★ (sc, ch 2, sc) in corner ch-2 sp, sc in each sc across to next corner ch-2 sp; repeat from ★ 2 times **more**; join with slip st to Back Loop Only of first sc.

Rnd 3: Ch 3, working in Back Loops Only, 2 dc in next ch, ch 2, 2 dc in next ch, ★ dc in each sc across to next corner ch-2, 2 dc in next ch, ch 2, 2 dc in next ch; repeat from ★ 2 times **more**, dc in each sc across; join with slip st to **both** loops of first dc.

Rnd 4: Ch 1, sc in both loops of same st and in each dc around working 3 sc in each corner ch-2 sp; join with slip st to first sc, finish off.

Square designed by Edna L. Neuhart.

#4 *Continued from page 9.*

EDGING

Rnd 1: With **right** side facing, join yarn with slip st in center sc of any corner 3-sc group; ch 3, 2 dc in same st, ★ † 2 dc in next sc, dc in next 25 sc, dc in same st as joining on same Square and in same st as joining on next Square, (dc in next 26 sc, dc in same st as joining on same Square and in same st as joining on next Square) across to last Square, dc in next 25 sc, 2 dc in next sc †, 3 dc in next sc; repeat from ★ 2 times **more**, then repeat from † to † once; join with slip st to first dc: 796 dc.

Rnd 2: Ch 3, dc in same st, ★ † dc in next dc, work FPtr around same st, dc in same st, 2 dc in next dc, dc in next 3 dc, work FPtr around next dc, (dc in next 6 dc, work FPtr around next dc) across to within 3 dc of next corner 3-dc group, dc in next 3 dc †, 2 dc in next dc; repeat from ★ 2 times **more**, then repeat from † to † once; join with slip st to first dc.

Rnd 3: Ch 1, sc in same st and in next 2 dc, 3 sc in next FPtr, ★ sc in next dc and in each st across to next corner FPtr, 3 sc in corner FPtr; repeat from ★ 2 times **more**, sc in next dc and in each st across; join with slip st to first sc, finish off.

Square designed by Duaine G. Olson.

#5 *Continued from page 11.*

Rnd 7: With **right** side facing, join Lt Blue with sc in center sc of any corner 3-sc group *(see Joining With Sc, page 1)*; sc in same st and in each sc across to center sc of next corner 3-sc group, ★ 3 sc in center sc, sc in next sc and in each sc across to center sc of next corner 3-sc group; repeat from ★ 2 times **more**, sc in same st as first sc; join with slip st to first sc: 84 sc.

Rnd 8: Slip st in Front Loop Only of same st and in each sc around *(Fig. 2, page 1)*; join with slip st to **both** loops of first slip st.

Rnd 9: Ch 1, working in free loops of sc on Rnd 7 *(Fig. 3a, page 2)*, sc in same st, ★ † skip next st, 7 dc in next st, skip next 2 sts, sc in next st, skip next 2 sts, 7 dc in next st, skip next st, pull up a loop in each of next 2 sts, YO and draw through all 3 loops on hook, skip next st, 7 dc in next st, skip next 2 sts, sc in next st, skip next 2 sts, 7 dc in next st, skip next st †, sc in next st; repeat from ★ 2 times **more**, then repeat from † to † once; join with slip st to first sc, finish off: 128 sts.

Rnd 10: With **right** side facing and working in Back Loops Only, join White with slip st in center dc of first 7-dc group; ★ † (ch 1, work Star, ch 3, slip st in next dc) 3 times, sc in next dc, ch 1, dc in next dc, ch 1, tr in next dc, ch 1, dtr in next sc, ch 1, tr in next dc, ch 1, dc in next dc, ch 1, sc in next dc †, slip st in next dc; repeat from ★ 2 times **more**, then repeat from † to † once; join with slip st to first slip st, finish off: 12 Stars.

SQUARE B (Make 24)

Rnds 1-4: With Lt Blue, work same as Square A, page 11: 24 ch-2 sps.

Rnds 5 and 6: Work same as Square A: 76 sc.

Rnds 7-9: With Blue, work same as Square A: 128 sts.

Rnd 10: Work same as Square A: 12 Stars.

ASSEMBLY

With White, alternating Squares, and working through **both** loops, whipstitch Squares together forming 6 vertical Strips of 8 Squares each *(Fig. 5a, page 2)*, beginning in first corner dtr and ending in next corner dtr; then whipstitch strips together in same manner.

EDGING

Rnd 1: With **right** side facing, join White with dc in any corner dtr; ch 5, dc in same st, ★ † work 32 dc evenly spaced across same Square, work 33 dc evenly spaced across each Square across to last Square, work 32 dc evenly spaced across last Square to corner dtr †, (dc, ch 5, dc) in corner dtr; repeat from ★ 2 times **more**, then repeat from † to † once; join with slip st to first dc: 924 dc.

Rnd 2: Ch 1, sc in same st, 3 sc in next corner ch-5 sp, ★ sc in each dc across to next corner ch-5 sp, 3 sc in corner ch-5 sp; repeat from ★ 2 times **more**, sc in each dc across; join with slip st to first sc, finish off: 936 sc.

Rnd 3: With **right** side facing, join Blue with sc in center sc of any corner 3-sc group; sc in same st and in each sc across to center sc of next corner 3-sc group, ★ 3 sc in center sc, sc in next sc and in each sc across to center sc of next corner 3-sc group; repeat from ★ 2 times **more**, sc in same st as first sc; join with slip st to first sc: 944 sc.

Rnd 4: Slip st in Front Loop Only of same st and in each sc around; join with slip st to **both** loops of first slip st, do **not** finish off.

Continued on page 45.

Rnd 5: Ch 1, working in free loops of sc on Rnd 3, sc in same st, ★ † skip next 2 sts, 7 dc in next st, (skip next 2 sts, sc in next st, skip next 2 sts, 7 dc in next st) across to next corner 3-sc group, skip next st †, sc in next st; repeat from ★ 2 times **more**, then repeat from † to † once; join with slip st to first sc, finish off.

Rnd 6: With **right** side facing and working in Back Loops Only, join White with slip st in center dc of first 7-dc group; ★ † (ch 1, work Star, ch 3, slip st in next dc) across to within 3 dc of next corner sc, sc in next dc, ch 1, dc in next dc, ch 1, tr in next dc, ch 1, dtr in next sc, ch 1, tr in next dc, ch 1, dc in next dc, ch 1, sc in next dc †, slip st in next dc; repeat from ★ 2 times **more**, then repeat from † to † once; join with slip st to first slip st, finish off.

Square designed by Rita Goshorn.

#6 *Continued from page 13.*

Rnd 3: With **right** side facing, join Green with sc in second sc of any corner 2-sc group; 2 sc in same st, ch 1, (skip next sc, sc in next sc, ch 1) across to next corner 2-sc group, skip next sc, ★ 3 sc in next sc, ch 1, (skip next sc, sc in next sc, ch 1) across to next corner 2-sc group, skip next sc; repeat from ★ 2 times **more**; join with slip st to first sc, finish off: 40 sc and 32 ch-1 sps.

Rnd 4: With **right** side facing, join White with sc in center sc of any corner 3-sc group; sc in same st, ch 1, (sc in next ch-1 sp, ch 1) across to next corner 3-sc group, skip next sc, ★ 3 sc in next sc, ch 1, (sc in next ch-1 sp, ch 1) across to next corner 3-sc group, skip next sc; repeat from ★ 2 times **more**, sc in same st as first sc; join with slip st to first sc: 44 sc and 36 ch-1 sps.

Rnd 5: Ch 1, 3 sc in same st, ch 1, (sc in next ch-1 sp, ch 1) across to next corner 3-sc group, skip next sc, ★ 3 sc in next sc, ch 1, (sc in next ch-1 sp, ch 1) across to next corner 3-sc group, skip next sc; repeat from ★ 2 times **more**; join with slip st to first sc, finish off: 48 sc and 40 ch-1 sps.

Rnd 6: With **right** side facing, join Green with sc in center sc of any corner 3-sc group; 2 sc in same st, ch 1, (sc in next ch-1 sp, ch 1) across to next corner 3-sc group, skip next sc, ★ 3 sc in next sc, ch 1, (sc in next ch-1 sp, ch 1) across to next corner 3-sc group, skip next sc; repeat from ★ 2 times **more**; join with slip st to first sc, finish off: 52 sc and 44 ch-1 sps.

Rnds 7 and 8: Repeat Rnds 4 and 5: 60 sc and 52 ch-1 sps.

ASSEMBLY

With White, randomly placing Squares as desired, and working through **both** loops, whipstitch Squares together forming 6 vertical strips of 8 Squares each **(Fig. 5a, page 2)**, beginning in center sc of first corner 3-sc group and ending in center sc of next corner 3-sc group; then whipstitch strips together in same manner.

EDGING

Rnd 1: With **right** side facing, join Green with sc in center sc of any corner 3-sc group; sc in same st, ch 1, (sc in next ch-1 sp, ch 1) 13 times, † sc in same st as joining on same Square, ch 1, sc in same st as joining on next Square, ch 1, (sc in next ch-1 sp, ch 1) 13 times †, repeat from † to † across to next corner 3-sc group, skip next sc, ★ 3 sc in next sc, ch 1, (sc in next ch-1 sp, ch 1) 13 times, repeat from † to † across to next corner 3-sc group, skip next sc; repeat from ★ 2 times **more**, sc in same st as first sc; join with slip st to first sc: 424 sc and 416 ch-1 sps.

Rnds 2-4: Ch 1, 2 sc in same st, ch 1, (sc in next ch-1 sp, ch 1) across to next corner 3-sc group, skip next sc, ★ 3 sc in next sc, ch 1, (sc in next ch-1 sp, ch 1) across to next corner 3-sc group, skip next sc; repeat from ★ 2 times **more**, sc in same st as first sc; join with slip st to first sc.

Finish off.

Square designed by Judith Gayler.

#7 *Continued from page 15.*

EDGING

Rnd 1: With **right** side facing, join Teal with sc in any corner;سc in same st, working in sts and across end of rows, ★ † work 33 sc evenly spaced across first Square, work 34 sc evenly spaced across each Square across †, 3 sc in corner; repeat from ★ 2 times **more**, then repeat from † to † once, sc in same st as first sc; join with slip st to first sc: 960 sc.

Rnd 2: Ch 1, (sc, ch 1) twice in same st, ★ † skip next sc, (sc in next sc, ch 1, skip next sc) across to center sc of next corner 3-sc group †, (sc, ch 1) twice in center sc; repeat from ★ 2 times **more**, then repeat from † to † once; join with slip st to first sc, finish off.

Rnd 3: With **right** side facing, join Purple with sc in any corner ch-1 sp; ch 1, sc in same sp, ch 1, (sc in next ch-1 sp, ch 1) across to next corner ch-1 sp, ★ (sc, ch 1) twice in corner ch-1 sp, (sc in next ch-1 sp, ch 1) across to next corner ch-1 sp; repeat from ★ 2 times **more**; join with slip st to first sc.

Rnd 4: Slip st in first corner ch-1 sp, ch 1, (sc in same sp, ch 1) twice, (sc in next ch-1 sp, ch 1) across to next corner ch-1 sp, ★ (sc, ch 1) twice in corner ch-1 sp, (sc in next ch-1 sp, ch 1) across to next corner ch-1 sp; repeat from ★ 2 times **more**; join with slip st to first sc, finish off.

Rnds 5 and 6: With Rose, repeat Rnds 3 and 4.

Square designed by Julene S. Watson.